Chunja's Nanjing

Chunja's Nanjing

Published in 2022 by Seoul Selection U.S.A., Inc.
4199 Campus Drive, Suite 550, Irvine, CA 92612
Phone: 949-509-6584 / Seoul office: 82-2-734-9567
Fax: 949-509-6599 / Seoul office: 82-2-734-9562
Email: hankinseoul@gmail.com
Website: www.seoulselection.com

ISBN: 978-1-62412-146-3
Printed in the Republic of Korea
The Work is published under the support of Literature Translation
Institute of Korea (LTI Korea).

Chunja's Nanjing

Kim Hyeok

Translated by

Stella Kim

Seoul Selection

Contents

Part I

Part II

Part III

Part I

Botchan Karakuri Clock

White tea utensils lay on a black lacquer tea table. Next to it stood a tea kettle full of water being boiled. Wearing a kimono patterned with Japanese iris, Haruko kneeled in front of the tea table. There were several cats lolling around her with their paws and tails tucked under them. Like the cats in traditional ukiyo-e woodblock prints, they sat still without moving a muscle.

When the water in the kettle finished boiling, Haruko poured it into two teacups to warm them up. A stream of water burbled into the cup, and a cat sitting under the table pricked up its ears at the sound. Holding the rolled-up cuff of her kimono with one hand, Haruko picked up a bamboo tea spoon with her other hand to scoop up tea leaves and put them into the kettle. When the teacups were warmed up, she poured the water into the drain and waited for the tea leaves to steep.

Both Haruko and the cats sat motionless. It took a long time for the tea to finish brewing, but Haruko wasn't bored. The perfect tea for the day was made by adjusting the boiling time depending on the tea leaves and the weather. Since she had to monitor everything so closely, she didn't have time to feel bored.

Bone-dry leaves came alive in the tea kettle, revealing their deep green color. The whole room was suddenly filled with the robust fragrance of tea. The scent rippled over the tatami mats and the wallpapered walls, reaching the ceiling and finally squirming out through the cracks between the sliding door and into the hallway.

Haruko's grandfather, who had been sitting upright and very still, flinched his shoulders. The upturned points of his Kaiser mustache twitched. One of the cats got up, placed its two front paws on the tatami mat, and stretched.

Haruko lifted the lid of the tea kettle. It was full of soggy tea leaves. She closed the lid again. At the soft clatter of the lid on the kettle, the cats pricked up their ears.

Haruko wrapped a silk cloth around the tea kettle,

picked it up, and poured tea into the cups. She held the kettle at just the right height: too low and it would touch the cup; too high and the tea would splash.

The soft murmur of water trickling into the cups was a treat for the ears. Enjoying the sound of the liquid was also part of the "way of tea." The cats turned their ears to where the sound was coming from, as if they were also enjoying the way of tea.

Haruko picked up the teacup. Making sure not to pass it over the steaming tea kettle, she carefully placed it on the table. "Bend your wrist so that the teacup doesn't pass directly over the tea kettle." Remembering the words of her teacher, she placed the teacup in front of Grandpa.

Then she looked up at him.

Grandpa stroked his Kaiser mustache with his right forefinger. Through this somewhat exaggerated motion, he was expressing solemnness, and it was something he often did as a habit. He lifted the teacup from the table and brought it to his lips. Then he tilted it toward his mouth.

Welcoming the subtle fragrance, he took a sip. Haruko watched him with a smile on her face, and a dimple formed near her lips.

"Mmm," Grandpa let out a moan.

"Grandpa, I told you you're not supposed to make a sound when drinking tea," said Haruko, her voice brimming with charm as she eyed him sideways. "When drinking tea, you must sit upright. You mustn't stare at the person sitting in front of you. You must speak quietly, with a pause after another person has finished talking. You should use both hands to lift the teacup to show respect, and you should not make a sound when drinking tea."

Haruko recited the tea ceremony etiquette she'd learned.

"Well, Princess Haruko, when I took a sip, it tasted dryer than I thought it would be."

With a mischievous smile in his eyes, Grandpa scrunched up his nose at her.

"It's Chinese pu-erh tea."

Grandpa's mustache twitched. "Chinese tea? Why Chinese of all things?"

"I had it specially brought over here," said Haruko as she held up the Chinese label on the tea container. "The Qianlong Emperor loved to drink it apparently. He was the longest-lived Chinese emperor. So live long like he did, Grandpa."

Haruko shuffled around the tea table on her knees toward him.

She said, "It may be a bit dry, but they say it's good for asthma. And you have bad lungs. I've been telling you to quit smoking."

She pouted her lips and pulled the pipe away from Grandpa. Laughing, he indulged her. He picked up a cat lying by his feet instead and stroked its head.

There were a lot of cats in his room. It wasn't just one or two, but more like a dozen. They were a breed native to Japan with black spots on white fur, short and stubby tails, triangular heads, and big pointed ears.

Grandpa petted the cat, gazing at it lovingly, the same way he looked at his granddaughter.

The wooden pipe that, at a glance, resembled a thin hammer, was polished like a bone, as Grandpa was a big smoker. There were also Chinese characters etched on the side of the pipe, although they were almost completely faded. There were two characters, one of which was "金," meaning gold. The other had faded so much that it was difficult to decipher.

"What does it say on your pipe?" Haruko asked,

staring at the characters. She'd seen him using the pipe all the time, but only today had she noticed the letters etched onto the side.

"That pipe is older than you, you know," Grandpa evaded an answer.

"The characters. The characters on your pipe."

"In fact, it's even older than your mother," he said with a long sigh. He was still not answering her question.

Haruko held the pipe in her hands and handed it back to Grandpa. He put the empty pipe up to his lips and pretended to smoke.

"You're adorable, Grandpa."

Watching him suck loudly on the empty pipe for an imaginary puff, Haruko smiled and flashed a dimpled smile.

Grandpa pulled the pipe out of his mouth and asked in all seriousness, "You'll be staying the night, won't you, princess?"

"Actually, I have to head back home. I have a lot of schoolwork to catch up on."

Grandpa's face clouded over in disappointment. "Why did you even come if you were going to leave so soon?"

"But we had a great time today! I even held a tea

ceremony for you. Wasn't that great, Grandpa?"
Haruko flung her arms around his neck.

"I'll finish learning the tea ceremony and come visit
you again, Grandpa," she cajoled him as if she were
talking to a sullen child. Then she looked at him and
moved her lips ever so slightly to say something, but
held her tongue and swallowed down the words that had
climbed all the way up her throat.

"Is something wrong?" asked Grandpa, reading the
expression on her face.

"Oh, it's nothing." Haruko once again swallowed
the words that had nearly reached her tongue. Afraid
Grandpa might see her true feelings on her face, she
hugged one of the cats in her arms and rubbed her cheek
against its round head. Then she looked into its large,
round eyes and said, "Take care of Grandpa for me, cats."

Having changed out of her kimono and back into her
everyday clothes, Haruko got ready to leave.

A cat mewed at her feet.

"You should drink the pu-erh tea," Haruko pleaded
with Grandpa, who followed her out to the front door. "It
may taste dry, but it's good for asthma."

Haruko knew that her grandfather would stand

and watch her with eyes as round as a cat's until she disappeared from his sight. Feeling his eyes on the back of her head, she left the house and walked out of the front yard.

Once she was out of his view, she took out her cell phone and dialed a number as if she were signaling for help.

She saw Jonghyeok standing in front of a jewelry store. He was a head taller than most others, so it was easy to spot him even from afar. He was a handsome man.

"Sorry to make you wait so long, Jonghyeok."

The street was crowded, but regardless Haruko threw her arms around him and kissed him on the cheek. It was her way of consoling him for having to walk the streets alone all day long. His cheeks were cold from the early spring breeze, and Haruko cupped them with her hands.

"Did your grandfather like the tea?" Jonghyeok's first question was about her grandfather's reaction.

"Mhmm," Haruko mumbled with her hands still on his cheeks. Her voice was small as she muttered a brief assent under her breath.

"Did you tell him about us?"

"Not yet…" Her voice grew even smaller. "He was

disappointed that I had to leave so quickly. I'm a bad granddaughter, aren't I?"

Haruko grew glum.

"Hey, let's go to the hot spring," said Jonghyeok, seeing she felt down. "Can you be my guide?"

Jonghyeok was an elite student from Yanbian, one of the more backwoods prefectures in China. He had been chosen to study abroad at the University of Tokyo, the best university in Japan. He was working on a doctorate in literature, and Haruko was in the same department. The story of their blossoming love was rather romantic, befitting two literature students. Jonghyeok was a bookworm who had spent over thirty years with his nose buried in books; Haruko, who was just a year younger than him, had been the first to ask him out.

They first met by a pond at school. On that day, Jonghyeok had been sitting beside the water in a daze. The autumn was well on its way, and ginkgo leaves were scattered on the surface of the water. The yellow leaves floated about, as if bound for a watery grave. The pond had been beautiful all summer, but now the leaves were turning it into an eyesore.

The pond was called Sanshiro, named after the novel of the same title by Natsume Soseki, the best known and most admired writer in Japan.

Kim Jonghyeok had earned his master's degree with a comparative study on China's Lu Xun and Japan's Natsume Soseki, and he was continuing his research on Soseki at the University of Tokyo. He was deeply infatuated with the writer who had been dubbed the "most beloved writer in Japan for the past millennium" by the Japanese media.

Jonghyeok always came to this pond. He would sit quietly on the rocks by the water and read a book or take a walk around the edge. It had already been two years since he came to study in Japan, but he could never simply pass this pond by.

"Did you drop something in there?"

Jonghyeok had been staring into the pond, deep in thought, when the question nudged him back to reality. He turned slowly. A woman holding books to her chest was looking up at him curiously. It was Haruko.

"Did you drop your phone in there?"

"No, I'm just me-meditating," Jonghyeok stuttered, flustered.

"Oh, I see. You were just staring into the pond for a while, so I…" She ducked her head in embarrassment.

"Well, happy meditating then!"

She gave a slight nod and turned away, then said, "This pond, it's the one in Natsume Soseki's novel."

"Yeah," Jonghyeok nodded in response. "Thank you."

Haruko looked great in her school's traditional-style uniform. University students rarely wore uniforms now, but in the past they all had to wear one. The carefree autumn breeze was messing up her long black hair, which caressed her lily-white face. She had attractive dimples on her cheeks that caught the eyes of passersby.

The breeze had left a ginkgo leaf on her shoulder like an ornament. Jonghyeok felt the urge to reach out and pick it off. And this peculiar urge stayed with him until she vanished from his sight through the red-orange gates of the university. He suddenly thought that one of the books that she'd been hugging to her chest might have been Soseki's *The Grass Pillow*.

He wanted to believe that it was *The Grass Pillow*. It was a story about an artist who happens to visit a village in the countryside, where he encounters the villagers, becomes enraptured by the scenery, and is unable to

19

work on his art. The protagonist was a version of Soseki, conflicted between Western and Eastern cultures. Jonghyeok had read the book again recently and thought he faced a similar cultural conflict as a Korean student in Japan.

Suddenly realizing that all these thoughts in his head originated from a woman he'd never seen before, he knuckled himself in the head with his fist.

"I must be having a nervous breakdown or something from studying too hard," murmured Jonghyeok as he caught a ginkgo leaf fluttering down from the tree and alighting on his shoulder. It was rumored that Soseki wrote *The Grass Pillow* during a mental breakdown.

Jonghyeok ran into her again at a ramen place called Akamon, meaning Red Gate, located near the real Akamon, the main gate of the University of Tokyo. One of the major attractions in Tokyo and a symbol of the university, Akamon had been built to welcome the daughter of Tokugawa Ienari, the eleventh shogun of the Tokugawa Shogunate, on her wedding day. Like a new bride arriving at a new wonder, Jonghyeok had walked through the gate with the same anticipation in his heart when he first came to the university.

His usual at the ramen place was its signature dish, Akamon Ramen. It was a belly-warming spicy dish for Japanese cuisine, which often tasted sweet. As most of the diners were students, it only cost three hundred yen. For a Korean man who enjoyed the spicy dishes of his homeland, it was a rather enticing dish, both for the taste and price. On top of that, he hadn't had a chance to try many Japanese dishes, which was another reason he kept on coming back for it.

Ramen in steamy broth was the best meal on a bleak and windy autumn day, and it seemed that many other people thought the same because the restaurant was packed.

After waiting for a long while, Jonghyeok finally found a seat by the door.

"Oh, you're the guy from Sanshiro," Haruko said with a smile of recognition as she walked in. Jonghyeok embarrassedly nodded at her with a mouthful of ramen noodles. She smiled even wider, making dimples appear on her cheeks.

Akamon was overflowing with people. It was a tiny restaurant with just eight tables. Some students who felt too awkward to share a table with strangers placed their bowls on window sills and ate alone.

But a little while later, she came to Jonghyeok's table with a bowl of ramen in her hands.

"Can I sit here?" she asked with such confidence and certainty that Jonghyeok nodded without even a moment's thought.

"Su-sure. Have a seat."

Jonghyeok's first impression of Haruko was a "union of languid melancholy and unconcealed vivacity."[1] He thought this description of a character from a Soseki novel was perfect for her.

"My name is Kim Jonghyeok," he gathered his courage and said, feeling rather uncomfortable to be chewing noodles across from each other in silence. "I'm in the literature department."

"Oh? I'm in the same department. I'm Haruko."

Haruko stood up and bowed, brushing back a strand of hair that had escaped from behind her ear. Jonghyeok got up awkwardly and bowed in response.

Haruko. Someone who had the same name popped into his head for a moment.

Haruko was surprised when Jonghyeok told her that he was Korean-Chinese.

"Eh?" After that common Japanese expression of surprise, she said, "*Sugoi* (awesome)!" Then she told him she was from Matsuyama.

"Eh?" It was Jonghyeok's turn to be surprised. "You mean the city in Soseki's *Botchan*? Where Dogo Onsen is? One of the three most famous hot springs in Japan?"

"That's right," Haruko nodded. "You know a lot about my hometown. Dogo Onsen in Matsuyama."

Her dimples appeared occasionally, when she mouthed certain syllables. The way she enunciated the name of the city and her expression as she said it were infused with pride for her hometown. Waking from a spell cast by her dimples, Jonghyeok redirected his gaze and said, "I heard the Botchan Karakuri Clock is there too."

"How do you know so much about my hometown?" asked Haruko, her eyes full of curiosity.

"I'm a huge Soseki fan. My dissertation is about him too, so…"

"Ah, *sugoi*."

"I'm doing a comparative analysis of him and the Chinese author Lu Xun."

With the spoon in her mouth, Haruko chimed in. "I like Soseki too. My favorite of his works is *I Am a Cat*."

Jonghyeok was surprised that their conversations, the brief one at the pond and the one they were having now, always flowed to this one topic—Natsume Soseki.

"That's a novel that stares straight at human society through the eyes of a cat," said Jonghyeok. "It's one of his earlier works, but it already shows the level he'd reached as a writer."

"Oh, I haven't had a chance to read it carefully. I just…"

Jonghyeok stopped moving his chopsticks and waited for Haruko to finish her sentence.

"I read it because I like cats."

Haruko let out an embarrassed giggle. Her shoulders shook as she laughed, and her straight, jet-black hair swayed by her blossoming bosom under the uniform.

"I have cats at home," Haruko continued. "Had them since I was young. A lot of them."

"A lot? How many is a lot?"

"Don't be surprised. Twelve."

"Eh?" Jonghyeok couldn't hide his surprise.

"My Grandpa loves cats."

Another person who liked cats also popped up into his head.

"All of the cats we have at home are Japanese Bobtails," said Haruko, excited to be talking about cats.

"You know, Japanese b-o-b-t-a-i-l," Haruko spelled it out with dimples on her cheeks. "Bobtail. It's a breed recognized by the CFA, the Cat Fanciers' Association. With short tails and big ears. At home, we call them *maneki-neko*. You know, like the cat with a raised paw you see in stores. Oh, there's one over there."

Haruko pointed at a cat figurine on the counter. It was one of those battery-powered figurines that waved its front paw to the diners.

"People in my hometown believe that *maneki-neko* brings luck." She laughed with sheer delight, swinging her hand like the cat figurine. The peal of her laughter rang like a ramen spoon clanging against a porcelain bowl.

"I've actually read some of Lu Xun's work as well," she said, returning to their original topic of conversation as though she shared Jonghyeok's seriousness.

"Which ones?" he asked, and she tilted her head to one side.

"The one with... the man with the queue..."

Jonghyeok laughed this time. He said, "All of the male characters in Lu Xun's novels sport a queue, since it was the custom at the time in China."

Haruko blushed. Stirring the leftover noodles in the bowl with her chopsticks, she tried to think of the works she'd read. After a bit of hesitation, she explained, "You know, the... the one about the man who keeps on going to a tavern and drinks on credit... or something like that."

"You mean *Kong Yiji*?"

"Yes! *Kong Yiji!*"

Haruko shouted out of pure excitement, attracting the attention of everyone slurping ramen in the restaurant. A blush spread across her cheeks.

Jonghyeok tried to save her from embarrassment by making a joke.

"I suppose we can't eat on credit here."

"Of course not," said Haruko as she smiled, shrugging her shoulders. "The owner lady will get mad at us."

"I think highly of Soseki's literary world, because he suggests that the more uneasy society becomes, the more we have to look back on the value of life hidden inside and reflect on ourselves," Jonghyeok explained about his research, after swallowing a bite of noodles. He was back to his serious self. Haruko put her spoon down and listened intently.

"And the social contradictions that Lu Xun saw and wanted to fix are still being reproduced and repeated. In that sense, these two writers achieved a pioneering vision about the future in their works, seeing as they both concentrated for a long time on the contradictions and conflicts of the human world."

"*Sugoi!*" said Haruko, nodding.

"Going to see the Karakuri Clock is a dream of mine," said Jonghyeok, changing the subject out of concern that he had been too serious all night.

"Let's go together sometime," Haruko answered without hesitation, and this time Jonghyeok blushed at the word "together."

"What are some other works by Lu Xun?" she asked with interest. "Could you recommend some for me? I'd like to read them."

"Oh, I can rattle off a list. There's *The True Story of Ah Q*, which is one of his best-known works. His essays and other collections are great, too. I actually have most of them in Japanese, since I'm studying them."

"Can I borrow them from you?" asked Haruko.

Jonghyeok nodded, almost aggressively.

"Well, since you promised to lend me your books, your ramen's on me."

Haruko took money out of her wallet.

"Oh, no, I can…" said Jonghyeok as he got up from his chair, but Haruko flashed him a smile, holding a thousand-yen bill in her hand.

"I'm loaded," she said as she showed him one side of the bill. "Natsume Soseki's on here too."

A dignified portrait of Soseki was printed on the thousand-yen bill.

Before he even had a chance to stop her, Haruko walked over to the counter and paid for their meal.

"Boyfriend?" said the owner of the restaurant as she took Haruko's money.

"*Iie!*" said Haruko as she shook her head no.

"Why are you paying for his ramen if he's not your boyfriend?"

Her voice was loud enough for everyone in the restaurant to hear.

Haruko blushed and said, "I'm never coming back to Akamon for ramen."

"Eh? I suppose you'll be going to nicer restaurants for nicer meals now that you've got yourself a boyfriend!"

The lady let out a loud bark of laughter as though she were having fun teasing Haruko, and Haruko left the restaurant with her face burning hot. But soon her dimpled face appeared again on the other side of the window. She pressed her face to the window and gestured goodbye to Jonghyeok, raising a hand and moving it back and forth like a *maneki-neko*. His ramen had grown cold, but Jonghyeok ate it all, leaving an empty bowl behind him.

After that day, Haruko often came to see Jonghyeok to borrow *The True Story of Ah Q, Medicine, A Madman's Diary, Hometown*, and other works by Lu Xun. The two of them read Soseki's *I Am a Cat, The Gate,* and *The Grass Pillow* together.

While the ginkgo trees around Sanshiro Pond changed colors and shed leaves several times, Jonghyeok and Haruko grew closer until they couldn't live without each other. It was as if Soseki had brought them together, and *maneki-neko* had brought them the luck of love. After he became accustomed to life in Japan, Jonghyeok learned that Japanese women never paid the bill in restaurants when dining with a man so as not to injure his pride. Helping others save face was the culture in Japan, the polite thing to do.

It took Jonghyeok four years from the day Haruko suggested they visit the Botchan Karakuri Clock together to actually come to the town where it stood. He'd already finished writing his dissertation.

"Did you have a tea ceremony with your Grandpa?" Jonghyeok asked, walking with one arm around Haruko's shoulder.

"I did. He liked it."

"And he's doing well?"

"Yeah. He has asthma, so he's been having a hard time. But what with the weather getting warmer, he's gotten much better."

"And he's taking walks and stuff?"

"*Mochirondayo* (of course)."

The two of them talked about Haruko's grandfather for a while. The closer he grew to Haruko, the more Jonghyeok realized that she talked a lot about her grandfather. She didn't just talk a lot about him—she always talked about him.

Soseki and cats were two of the topics she brought up most of the time, but even they paled in comparison to the number of times she mentioned her grandfather. Not a single day went by without her mentioning him at least once, and it seemed that he was almost a legendary figure to her.

She said he was over five feet, nine inches, tall. He was in his nineties yet still rode around on his bicycle. He still drank a liter of Japanese sake without blinking an eye. He once knocked down three young men who were drunk and making a scene at the hot springs with a single punch. He owned a pottery shop and would walk up and down the steps with a package of pottery tucked under each arm.

By Haruko's description, her grandfather sounded like one of the greatest warriors from the Edo shogunate. And above all, he adored Haruko.

Ever since she was young, he'd called her "Onsen Princess."

Looking into Haruko's beautiful face, with dimples appearing and vanishing like a rainbow, Jonghyeok asked, "How did such a beautiful princess end up with a student from China of all people?"

He'd assumed it was an evil inherent in Japan's patriarchal culture that beautiful and well-educated women have a difficult time finding husbands. But he was surprised when Haruko simply answered, "Because of Grandpa."

She added that her hot-tempered grandfather was the one preventing her from getting married. She'd brought home several boyfriends before, but they all ended up breaking up with her due to her grandfather's intrusive questions and abrupt interruptions.

But she couldn't *not* show her future husband to her grandfather either. He was the oldest member of her family, and, above all, he loved her very much.

Yet he was growing ever more difficult to please. He refused to accept Haruko's boyfriends because their families weren't prestigious enough or because they weren't educated enough, and he even turned one down because the boy said something in a regional dialect. They were all reasons to refuse those boyfriends as the future spouse of his beloved granddaughter. Her last boyfriend was rejected because he'd bleached his hair. He'd come back the next time with his hair dyed black again, but Grandpa stubbornly maintained his bias toward him.

Several days after Grandpa had rejected her boyfriend, Haruko and her boyfriend were walking through Akamon with their arms linked when someone stopped them dead in their tracks. Haruko nearly jumped out of her skin when she realized who it was. In perfect health in spite of his old age, Grandpa had traveled all the way to Tokyo to stop her from dating the boy he'd rejected.

"He's terrifying. Like an old yakuza boss."

That was what her boyfriend had said about Grandpa when he broke up with her.

Having listened to Haruko's explanation, Jonghyeok thought that perhaps the "unconcealed vivacity" and "languid melancholy" in her personality resulted from her grandfather's influence.

Haruko had meant to tell Grandpa about Jonghyeok on this visit, but she couldn't work up the courage when she actually faced him and ended up hesitating and dithering until she finally gave up. Jonghyeok had been waiting outside, nearly as anxious as Haruko.

Haruko looked at him and said, "I brewed him the pu-erh tea you gave me."

"Did he like it?"

"He said it was a bit dry." Haruko smiled quietly, remembering Grandpa's twitchy mustache. "But he did compliment me on my performance of the tea ceremony. Very highly."

Haruko had gotten interested in the tea ceremony while working part time at a cultural center near school. The cultural center not only offered tea ceremony lessons but also ran a small library for its members and hosted various music and art events. Haruko took up the tea ceremony as a way to train herself, although a part of her did it because it was a bit of a fad among young people. But there was another reason: Grandpa loved tea to the point of collecting all kinds of tea utensils.

Haruko became fascinated with the tea ceremony, and she even taught Jonghyeok what she'd learned. Every day, she talked about tea and tea ceremony. Once, she'd explained to him the ceremony's origin.

"People drank water to satisfy their physiological need to relieve thirst. Then they started looking for better tasting beverages. But in drinking tea, the Japanese people didn't stop at appreciating the taste of the tea. Instead, they decided on a rather strict process of brewing and serving it, as well as on manufacturing the tools used to brew and drink it. And they imparted meaning to each step of the process.

"Carefully making a fire, boiling water, brewing tea to the optimal taste, and then drinking it may be ordinary daily actions, but that series of ordinary actions is only possible when we set our minds to it. That was why our ancestors considered it a ritual and called it 'tea ceremony.' When we drink tea in such a reverential manner, our hearts find solitude, and we become aware of the importance of other people in our lives. Furthermore, it makes our hearts more peaceful, which helps us achieve the spirit of 'peace' that binds together the Japanese people."

Haruko was infatuated with this traditional rite. And Jonghyeok was proud of her intense interest in a single topic.

"You know, the Japanese tea ceremony actually came from Buddhist monks who were studying abroad in China," explained Haruko, one day after she returned from the cultural center.

"The Japanese tea ceremony originated with the Japanese Buddhist monk Eisai, who studied in China in the twelfth century, and they say that it all goes back to the spirit of China's Chan School of Buddhism. And the schools of tea ceremony that were founded by the descendants of Sen Rikyu are the mainstream tea ceremonies practiced in Japan today. They're the San

Senke, which can be traced back to the three sons of Sen Sotan, the son of Sen Rikyu's second wife. So Sen Rikyu's three grandsons, born to his stepson, continued the family tradition. Sen Rikyu's first grandson founded Omotesenke; the second grandson, Mushakojisenke; and the third grandson, Urasenke. And..."

"Goodness, it's hard to drink a cup of tea around here," Jonghyeok interrupted Haruko, unable to wait any longer after listening considerately for a while. "I'm just going to drink coffee."

Haruko laughed sheepishly and mixed a cup of instant coffee for him. But even as she handed him the cup, she continued her lecture on the tea ceremony.

As Jonghyeok sipped on coffee and Haruko on green tea, their conversation continued.

"Japanese culture doesn't allow stepping out of line. It needs everything to fit perfectly within a designed frame and can't handle anything that deviates from that form. Everything that comes to Japan is precisely measured and standardized and ends up losing even the tiniest bit of irregularity or room for exception. That's the typical characteristic of Japanese culture. And that's how the spirit of tea that came from China has continued in Japan in the form of the tea ceremony."

Jonghyeok put down his coffee cup and responded, "We're a bit different. The typical characteristic of Chinese culture is that everything is related to the way we lead our lives. One example of Chinese culture is that things aren't limited to a particular place or time. When you go to rural villages in China, you can see people freely drinking and eating out of their bowls in the streets. People drink a lot of tea, but there's no particular ritual or procedure they follow. And we ethnic Koreans in China are also different. We don't really have the habit of drinking tea like the Chinese. So young people these days are more used to drinking Western beverages, like coffee or Coke. I don't see dietary habits as something lofty that's separate from daily life. Wouldn't it be ridiculous if you couldn't get to the essence of something because it's trapped inside complicated formalities?"

"Huh? Wait, is this your way of mocking me for talking so much about the tea ceremony when I don't understand the essence of it?"

"Oh, no, not at all! Do you know how adorable you are when you talk about the tea ceremony?"

Jonghyeok pulled Haruko into his arms and kissed her

on her dimple. The two were deeply in love despite the cultural differences that occasionally rose to the surface.

Onsen Station was quite far from Grandpa's house. Yet Jonghyeok and Haruko walked to the station without even thinking to take the train, all the while talking about Grandpa.

Dogo Onsen was certainly Matsuyama's iconic attraction. It was the hot spring with three thousand years of history that Soseki praised in *Botchan*: "While there was nothing in this town which compared favorably with Tokyo, the hot springs were worthy of praise."[2] It was also known as an imperial hot spring, visited by Japanese emperors. Poets and artists were also said to have frequented it as well.

"They say that when a white heron put its injured leg into the hot water gushing from a crevice, it was completely healed. That's how these hot springs came to be famous."

Haruko had told Jonghyeok about the legend behind the hot springs in her hometown on the yellow tram from Matsuyama Station to Grandpa's house earlier that morning. The legend was as beautiful as the town itself.

Jade-colored roofs resembling battle helmets peeked

through the gaps between magnificent buildings on the streets, which were packed with local shops and restaurants. There were many seafood restaurants and udon noodle bars, where people lined up for a bite to eat. Artisan shops were also crowded with customers. The various inns and hotels along the streets were proof that the town was a famous tourist destination. Every corner of the town emanated an aura of vintage beauty.

Among the variety of food served everywhere, "Botchan *dan-go*," which were little balls of sweet rice cake known to have been favored by the main character, were making people's mouths water.

After tasting some Botchan *dan-go*, Haruko picked up some small cakes. She popped one into Jonghyeok's mouth. Filled with red-bean paste, the cake flooded Jonghyeok's mouth with pleasant sweetness.

"It's called *taruto*," Haruko explained. "Apparently, the lord of Matsuyama liked it so much that he learned to make them himself. How is it? Good?"

With his mouth full of *taruto*, Jonghyeok nodded at Haruko, who let out a peal of laughter. She then picked crumbs off the corner of his mouth and put them in her own.

Walking through the streets eating *taruto*, they gradually recovered their cheerful composure after a morning full of anxiety and worry. They'd booked rather late return tickets because they wanted to see the Botchan Karakuri Clock. They'd passed by it in the morning but didn't have time to enjoy it as they were on their way to see Haruko's grandfather. Both of them had been much too anxious about telling him about their relationship to dillydally by the clock.

Still full of traces of the Meiji era as well as footprints of famous writers and artists, various parts of the town emanated with the subtle fragrance of literature and art. This was also the place where Haruko, Jonghyeok's love and the woman who had a "union of languid melancholy and unconcealed vivacity," had been born.

Feeling content, Jonghyeok pulled Haruko closer to him.

The clock was the one that featured in Soseki's novel *Botchan*, a semi-autobiographical coming-of-age story based on Soseki's childhood experiences and his year as an English teacher at Matsuyama Middle School. It was known for vivid descriptions of Matsuyama and its people during the Meiji era.

Each hour, Karakuri Clock came to life, and characters from the novel emerged to act out scenes from the story. Along with the hot springs, the clock was now a famous tourist attraction in town.

Jonghyeok came to Dogo Onsen feeling rather desperate. He wasn't there for a nice bath but rather to find traces of Soseki's times and works from the hot spring that Soseki and Botchan, the protagonist of his novel, had visited every day, carrying a red towel. Jonghyeok and Haruko stopped in front of the main bathhouse at Dogo Onsen, which had a tiled roof resembling the wings of a white heron about to take off.

"It's a cultural heritage," said Haruko, gladly playing the tour guide. "The first public bathhouse to be designated as a National Important Cultural Property."

The largest crowd, however, was gathered in front of the Karakuri Clock, which had been erected twenty years ago to celebrate the hundredth anniversary of the establishment of the Dogo Onsen bathhouse's main building. Models dressed in kimonos like the characters in the novel were leisurely walking around the clock with parasols, posing with visitors for pictures in front of the clock. Everyone anxiously checked their watches and cell phones, waiting for the top of the hour when the characters of *Botchan* would emerge from the elaborate clock, which had cost a total of one billion yen to build.

There was a small spring next to the clock. Etched with the characters "Hojoen," it was a footbath, filled with spring water flowing out of a huge water cauldron from the Meiji era. Many people were sitting on the bench that encircled the spring, with their feet in the warm water.

"Let's go for a footbath," said Haruko as she led Jonghyeok by the hand. Placing her hand on Jonghyeok's shoulder, she whispered, "It's free of charge."

The two of them sat on the bench and placed their feet in the warm water. Heat rose from the water, creating a haze, and Haruko's feet looked as white as bamboo shoots. Jonghyeok thought they were beautiful. They sat side by side and enjoyed the footbath, which seemed to wipe away their fatigue and worries. With his feet still in the footbath, Jonghyeok absently looked at his wristwatch. Then he looked over at the Karakuri Clock.

It was 2:54. He only needed to wait a few more minutes.

Suddenly he felt something on his shoulder. Something had struck him. A sharp pain spread across his shoulder for a moment. He noticed that the heavy object that was still on his shoulder was a cane. Jonghyeok turned around in shock to see an old man standing behind him. He was wearing a dark black kimono with a pair of white *tabi* socks and *zori* sandals. In his traditional Japanese attire, the old man looked haughty and even bizarre among the casually dressed visitors in town. The bluish dark circles forming a half-moon under his eyes looked particularly prominent. The tall old man held up the cane and pointed it at Jonghyeok's face, close enough to almost touch his nose. Twitching his white mustache, he asked in a loud and high-pitched voice, "Who the hell are you?"

As if a camera had suddenly zoomed in on the old man, he had appeared in front of Jonghyeok out of the blue and was honking at him like a goose. Flustered, Jonghyeok managed to say, "I'm a student… just visiting."

The old man then pointed his cane at Haruko and yelled, "What are you doing with her?"

But before Jonghyeok even had a chance to answer, he asked, "What do you think you're playing at, sitting next to her!"

"She's my girlfriend," answered Jonghyeok, despite his bewilderment. The old man was questioning him rudely, so Jonghyeok answered almost defiantly.

"What did you say?"

The old man's face hardened immediately. The muscle in his jaw bulged as he clenched his teeth. Outraged, the old man held up his cane high and brought it down on Jonghyeok. Jonghyeok held up his arms to brace himself for another blow when Haruko jumped out of the footbath and grabbed the cane. Tourists stopped by to watch a barefooted young woman and an old man in a traditional kimono pulling on a cane as if engaged in a tug-of-war.

"Please stop, Ojiisan!"

Haruko's voice tore through the air like the sound of silk fabric ripping.

"Huh? Grandpa?"

Jonghyeok's eyes widened like two flashes of light. Only then did he realize the identity of this eccentric old man with eyebrows like those of the giant gatekeepers standing guard at the entrance of Buddhist temples. He was finally face to face with the legendary Grandpa whom Haruko had always mentioned.

Without even putting his shoes back on, Jonghyeok rushed out of the footbath and bowed to Haruko's grandfather.

"It's a pleasure to meet you, sir!"

The old man lowered his cane.

"I'm sorry, sir," Jonghyeok apologized. "I didn't recognize who you were. My name is Kim Jonghyeok, and I'm studying at the University of Tokyo."

Haruko's grandfather placed both hands on top of the cane. Huffing and puffing, he looked around with cold piercing eyes at the people gathered around them. His mustache and eyebrows twitched.

"What the hell are you all looking at? Aren't there better sights to see at Dogo Onsen than this?"

At his tongue-lashing, the embarrassed onlookers began to scatter.

Grandpa raised a thumb and brushed each side of his mustache.

"Who did you say you were?" he asked.

"My name is Kim Jonghyeok. I came from China to study literature at the University of Tokyo."

Jonghyeok even told him what he was studying at the university, like a new student feeling daunted and nervous in front of an upperclassman about to scold him.

"That's not important. What are you doing with

Haruko?"

Jonghyeok looked over at Haruko, whose face had turned as white as the traditional Japanese paper *washi*.

"Ojiisan, why don't we go to that tea room over there to talk. It's cold outside?" she pleaded, linking her arm with her grandfather's. But he shook her off rather roughly, making Haruko stumble a bit.

"What's your relationship with Haruko?" he asked Jonghyeok.

After a moment's hesitation, Jonghyeok replied in a voice that was louder and clearer than before, "We're dating."

"Dating?"

The upward-pointing ends of Grandpa's Kaiser mustache trembled.

"With whose permission?" Grandpa roared with anger once again. His piercing voice rang through the square in front of the station. People were still watching them from a distance.

Momentarily, Jonghyeok was at a loss for words. He was thrown by the question that the old man had asked as though it were his right.

"Was that man the reason you hurried off?" Grandpa

asked Haruko this time. "You left me and the cats after a halfhearted tea ceremony because of that *kakashi* (scarecrow)?"

"No, Grandpa!" Haruko answered hastily, a low and urgent voice emerging from under her tongue. "I was going to introduce him to you..."

Haruko studied his face out of the corner of her eyes and saw that Grandpa's eyes were quivering, his opaque pupils full of rancor.

"And you," Grandpa said, turning to Jonghyeok once again. "Where did you say you were from?"

He angrily brushed over his mustache with his thumb again.

"I'm from China," Jonghyeok answered.

Grandpa's mustache trembled again.

"Then you're a Chink?"

Jonghyeok jerked his head up and looked at Haruko's grandfather, surprised at the derogatory word. He was intimidated by the old man's twitching face but spoke up clearly.

"Yes, I'm from China."

Grandpa lifted his cane and slammed it down on the ground.

"Ahem!" he loudly cleared his throat and turned away from Jonghyeok, brushing the skirt of his kimono to the side. And without even turning his head, he spoke to Haruko, or perhaps to Jonghyeok. "I command you to break up!"

He then walked away, ramming his cane into the ground at every step.

Haruko looked at Jonghyeok, her face scrunched up like crumpled paper, about to burst into tears. Then her eyes turned to Grandpa's cold, broad back, moving farther away as the hem of his kimono flapped in the wind.

"Ojiisan!" she called to him. Her voice was mixed with tears. But Grandpa didn't even turn his head.

She ran after him, barefoot. Only then did Jonghyeok collect his shoes strewn about by the footbath and put them on. Flummoxed by what had just happened, he didn't even think to put his socks on. He then picked up Haruko's shoes and followed after her.

Clang!

As he took a step, he heard the clock bell chiming above his head. The bell rang from the corner of the square, and crowds of people shouted in excitement as they hurried over to the clock.

Jonghyeok turned his head toward the timepiece. It was announcing the top of the hour.

A Testimony in Spring

It had been a long time since Jonghyeok had been home. Even during his studies, he had returned home at least once a year during summer or winter break, but he hadn't been home for three years since beginning work on his dissertation. Now he was finally back in China, and this time he wasn't alone.

Outside Yanji Airport, Jonghyeok called a cab standing by in the airport square.

"To Rokgol, please."

Instead of heading to his parent's apartment in the city, Jonghyeok paid a much larger sum to head to his grandmother's home in Rokgol. When the cab drove into the city, Jonghyeok asked the driver to stop for a moment and rushed into a supermarket. When he returned, there were two cartons of cigarettes in his hands.

"Huh? What are you doing?" Haruko asked in surprise. "Are you going to take up smoking again?"

Jonghyeok had reluctantly quit at Haruko's unrelenting request. It was the power of love that enabled him to quit.

"No, it's a gift," said Jonghyeok as he stuffed the cartons into his luggage.

"You're not going to just do as you please now that you're back home, are you? Taking up smoking again and stuff?"

Haruko's eyes were clouded with worry as she looked into Jonghyeok's face.

"Of course not," Jonghyeok replied as his loving gaze rested on Haruko's pouting lips. "These really are a gift."

The two of them had become a celebrity couple among their peers, as famous as Sanshiro Pond on campus. Their love grew ever deeper among the envy and admiration of their classmates.

On one of his birthdays in Japan, Jonghyeok once again realized how much Haruko loved him. Even he had forgotten his birthday, but Haruko hadn't. She'd made a reservation at a fancy restaurant and even handed him a gift: a cell phone case inscribed with his initials.

She also gave him a special treat—red bean rice.

"Have some," she said affectionately as she handed him a spoon. "You have to have some of this rice today. It's something you have to eat on your birthday."

Jonghyeok scooped up a spoonful of the red bean rice and brought it to his mouth. It was sticky and sweet.

Just as Koreans had seaweed soup on their birthdays, Japanese people ate red bean rice.

"It's red rice, called *sekihan*," said Haruko, watching Jonghyeok eat the treat with a smile on her face. She went on to tell him about how the Japanese came to eat *sekihan* on birthdays. "Japanese people always eat *sekihan* when a baby is born, or when there's something to celebrate, like a wedding."

Then lowering her voice, she said, "Mothers also give their daughters *sekihan* when they get their first period, too. It means they've become adults, and it's a subtle way to let the rest of the family know. It's a special dish that we eat on really important occasions."

Delicious food and a great present weren't all that Haruko had prepared for Jonghyeok's birthday.

Even after a drink and an ice cream, and a kiss that was stronger than liquor and sweeter than ice cream, Haruko's birthday surprises continued. She pulled out a book—Natsume Soseki's *Botchan*. Jonghyeok thought that it was a gift for him, but instead of handing him the book, she opened it and began to read aloud.

"When Red Shirt laughed, he laughed at my simplicity. My word! What chances have the simple-hearted or the pure in a society where they are made objects of contempt! Kiyo would never laugh at such a time; she would listen with profound respect. Kiyo is far superior to Red Shirt."[3]

Jonghyeok felt his mouth open in surprise. It wasn't the passage—he'd read *Botchan* so many times for his dissertation that he'd nearly become numb to how it had moved his heart. Instead, he was surprised because Haruko had just read the entire passage in Korean without missing a word and with flawless Korean intonation.

"Haruko, *sugoi* (that's great)!" Jonghyeok exclaimed in Japanese. "*Sugoi*, Haruko!"

"Why don't we speak only in Korean tonight?" Haruko suggested in Korean, as she put the book down. "And we have to drink a shot if we speak Japanese."

She said that she'd been secretly learning Korean to surprise Jonghyeok. One of the students learning the tea ceremony at the cultural center was from Korea, and Haruko had been learning Korean from her for over three months in addition to studying the tea ceremony. She'd never even hinted at it, and Jonghyeok was astonished as much by her ability to keep a secret for so long as by her ability to speak Korean.

"I have a Korean boyfriend, and if I really love him, I should at least learn the language he speaks, don't you think?" asked Haruko as she snuggled into Jonghyeok's arms. Touched by her considerate gesture, Jonghyeok held her tight in his arms.

"*Itai* (it hurts)!" Haruko blurted out in Japanese.

"*Itai*? Hah! You have to drink *bappai* (a penalty shot)!"

"Eh, *bappai*? Now you have to take a shot too!"

They poured each other a shot of fruit wine as a penalty for speaking Japanese.

Clink! The glasses bumped against each other, and the wine tasted sweeter than ever.

For spring break, Jonghyeok was heading home with his beloved Japanese girlfriend for the first time.

But a part of him was anxious. His first encounter with Haruko's grandfather at the hot springs had ended in unpleasantness. Although Haruko had chased after her grandfather barefoot and pleaded with him, he didn't give them his blessing. She ended up returning home crying. Helping her put her shoes back on her cold feet, Jonghyeok felt a chill of despondency run up his back.

Another obstacle they had to face was Jonghyeok's grandmother in China. Born in 1920, she was well in her nineties.

"Eh? Ninety-three? She's even older than my grandfather."

"She is. But she's in amazing health. She still carries around a good-sized bundle on her head."

"Ninety-three. I can't even imagine."

"Koreans refer to the age of ninety as *jolsu* or *dongni*. *Dongni* means frozen pear, because you get black spots on your face like those that appear on frozen pears. We eat a lot of frozen pears in the winter in my hometown."

"Oh really?"

"Have you had frozen pears before?"

"Yeah."

"My grandma's like a frozen pear. She's soft on the

inside, but like most elderly people, her appearance and her way of thinking are as hard as the outside of a frozen pear."

Jonghyeok's mother had worked for the women's movement for a long time as a member of the All-China Women's Federation and had Jonghyeok in her late thirties. Since she was busy with work, her son was raised by his grandmother. He went to elementary school in Rokgol, and when his mother came to take him to the city, he ran away to the cornfield. He hid there until twilight, watching the sun roll down off Deer Rock and crying, not wanting to be separated from his grandmother.

After he moved to the city, he always waited for breaks, when he would get to go to Rokgol and see her.

Every school break, Jonghyeok's bent-backed grandmother would walk out to the willow tree standing just outside the village. That was the spot where the bus that came every three days stopped to pick up or drop off passengers. She would wait under the tree until the bus brought Jonghyeok to the village.

When Jonghyeok visited, Grandma became the busiest person in the world. She would pull up her skirt and dig through the deep pockets in the loose pants underneath to produce candies, like magic. She would also save up the money she won by playing the *hwatu* card game with other old ladies in the village and give it to Jonghyeok as pocket money. Sometimes she fished through the chicken coop for fresh, warm eggs to hard-boil for him.

She also used to clean and polish a washbasin with a straw scrubber and the fine ash she'd collected from the kitchen furnace. Once it was clean and shiny, she would pump water into it and wash Jonghyeok's snotty face and his Communist Youth League uniform.

Jonghyeok loved his sprightly little grandmother with her stinging slaps and her sometimes sharp tongue.

Grandma adored him back, so much so that once she went all the way to the city for a surprise visit on his birthday and ended up getting hit by a car. The accident left her with a slight limp, but otherwise she was in great health for an old woman in her nineties. She was strong enough to walk around the village freely. Until just a few years ago, she did all the housework herself, making kimchi and fermenting soy sauce. She'd even been featured on a county radio show as a model example of an elderly woman.

Jonghyeok wanted her to move to the city and live with his mother, but Grandma said that Rokgol was her birthplace and would also be where she'd be buried. He'd paid a young woman in the village to care for Grandma for a few hours every day, but his stubborn Grandma had sent the girl away.

Grandma always missed Jonghyeok. When he was leaving for Japan, she traveled all the way from Rokgol to the city. That evening, Jonghyeok fell asleep by her side, holding her hand in his.

"I'll come live with you when I return home after finishing my studies," he'd told her, but she only smacked her lips on her toothless mouth and cried silent tears.

He'd been home twice since he'd left for Japan, but he only saw his grandmother on one occasion. That was already three years ago. Every time he called his mother, he would first ask about his grandmother even before saying a proper hello. His mother jokingly complained, "I'm nearly seventy, you know. But Grandma's the only old lady you ask for!"

The fact that his grandmother was still alive and well in her hometown was enough to make Jonghyeok happy.

One thing about her was that she strongly disliked

Japan. It wasn't particularly unusual because people her age had lived through the Japanese invasions of Korea and China. But her aversion to Japan and its people was surprising.

Once Jonghyeok's mother bought a flat-screen television and brought it all the way to Rokgol, but Grandma shook her head in refusal. Her face had hardened when she heard it was a Japanese brand. His mother ended up returning the TV and purchasing a Korean one instead.

"She's so stubborn," his mother had grumbled a little, but she always did whatever Grandma asked her to do.

Grandma came to visit Jonghyeok and his mother around New Year's Day for a few years when Jonghyeok was in middle school, and once, during a meal, she put down her spoon and stopped eating. She'd complimented Jonghyeok's mother about how the rice had been perfectly steamed. His mother had answered, "It's because of the rice cooker. It's a Japanese brand, and it's great!"

His mother had to cook another serving of rice in the old pot. She called Grandma "a fussy old woman," but to Jonghyeok, Grandma was just adorable. He couldn't really understand her extreme hatred of Japan, but he loved everything about her.

And here he was now, in love with a Japanese woman. In fact, he'd lied to Grandma about going to study in Japan and told her instead that he was going to Korea.

Before they decided to take this trip, Jonghyeok told Haruko about all of this. And they'd even planned to lie to Grandma—Jonghyeok was going to tell her that he'd met his girlfriend in Seoul. Fortunately, Haruko had grown fluent in Korean day after day, nearly to the point where she could fool people by pretending to be Korean. She was brilliant and beautiful, and Jonghyeok was helplessly in love with her.

"I'm sorry to ask so much of you," apologized Jonghyeok in the cab, after going over their plan and lies again. He grabbed her hand in his.

"What do we do if your *sobo* (grandmother) doesn't like me?"

Haruko's big eyes were full of worry. This was her first time in China. She'd bought yellow Amur Adonis blossoms to give to Jonghyeok's grandmother, as the flower was a symbol of longevity and blessing. She'd planned to bring a flower pot to the airport, but Jonghyeok had shaken his head no. Grandma knew a lot about flowers and plants in general, and he was sure that she'd notice the pot was from Japan.

"Do you think our love is something that our grandparents can't approve of?" Haruko asked with tears in her eyes.

Jonghyeok quickly wiped them away.

"Don't cry. You'll ruin your makeup. When she sees how pretty you are, I'm sure she'll approve."

But Haruko let out a sigh at Jonghyeok's effort to comfort her.

Watching the familiar scenery outside the window, Jonghyeok said, "But I don't blame her. Just like Kiyo and her grandmother in Soseki's *Botchan*, I spent more time with my grandma than my parents. You have no idea how much I cried when I read the scene where Kiyo's grandmother dies from pneumonia. I've never even imagined Grandma passing away."

"That's how I am with my grandfather," said Haruko, looking up at Jonghyeok. He rested his cheek against Haruko's lavender-scented hair. As if Haruko's sigh were contagious, he also let out a sigh.

The cab was filled with silence for a moment.

"You're both Japanese?" asked the gruff cab driver, who

had been driving quietly so far.

"No," Haruko answered in Korean, a little too insistently.

After about two hours, the cab finally arrived in Rokgol, or Deer Valley, named because there were a lot of deer living there. This remote rural village deep in a valley was where Jonghyeok had spent his childhood years.

As the cab drove along the village road, Haruko rolled down the window a bit. An unfamiliar scent brushed by on the wind. It was a smell that only first-time visitors could notice, and it made Haruko both a little nervous and a little excited. She was mesmerized by the rural scenery in this foreign land that was unfolding before her.

Cloud tails were caught on the top of distant mountain peaks, and a field at the foot of the mountains was speckled with slate-roofed rural houses in this quiet and peaceful village. The restrained beauty of the village almost looked like a still from a movie.

The cab slowly squeezed into a narrow alley between the fences of sorghum straw that surrounded every house and finally came to a stop in front of an old abode.

Jonghyeok hurried out of the cab, but then a look of bewilderment spread across his face. There was a van parked in front of his grandmother's house. About seven or eight people were gathered near it, talking in low voices.

Jonghyeok unloaded his luggage from the trunk and was paying the cab driver when he heard a surprised voice from among the small crowd.

"My goodness, Jonghyeok!"

A woman sporting horn-rimmed glasses approached Jonghyeok and Haruko.

"Mother!" Jonghyeok left the luggage on the ground and rushed over to embrace her.

"Mother?" Astonished, Haruko looked at the two of them.

"What are you doing here?" asked Jonghyeok's mother, with her arms wrapped around him. "You didn't even tell me you were coming! When did you get here?"

"Just now, actually."

At his words, she slapped his back lightly. "You didn't even stop by Yanji but came straight here to see Grandma first, didn't you?"

Jonghyeok then introduced Haruko, who had been

standing nervously, to his mother.

"Remember? I told you over the phone…"

Haruko bowed to Jonghyeok's mother, greeting her in Korean, "Nice to meet you, ma'am. My name is Haruko."

"Oh, you speak Korean!" Jonghyeok's mother looked closely at her, pleasantly surprised. "Pretty and good at Korean."

Having worked in the women's movement for all her life, Jonghyeok's mother had an ear for people's thoughts and an eye for character. She had been taken aback when Jonghyeok told her about his Japanese girlfriend but readily accepted his decision.

After greetings were exchanged, Jonghyeok asked his mother, "So what's going on? Who are those people?"

For a moment, his mother's eyes wavered in hesitation. Then determinedly, she said, "They're from South Korea."

"Why are they here?"

"They came to interview your grandmother."

"Is it another one of those "healthy elderly people" shows? Well, I guess she could be featured on that South Korean TV show, *Capture the Moment: How Is That Possible?*"

His mother gestured to the people near the van to

come over. Then she introduced Jonghyeok to them, proudly telling them that he was her son and was studying abroad.

Jonghyeok glanced at the business card that one of the people handed him. His eyebrows furrowed in confusion.

Coalition for Comfort Women Issues.

A woman in her forties, whose business card said she was a team leader at the coalition, stepped up and explained who they were to Jonghyeok.

"Every year, we interview and survey the survivors of Japan's wartime sexual slavery around the world, their families, and their living conditions. We're trying to collect basic data for health and welfare programs. We've been trying to improve our services and also identify new projects, which was what led us here to China. We came to visit your grandmother as part of a general survey of the surviving comfort women in China."

As he listened to her, Jonghyeok's mind went completely blank. His ears were ringing, and he couldn't hear anything.

For some reason, he looked over at Haruko. She stared back at him with a grave expression.

Jonghyeok opened the door carefully. He pulled the door up a little bit as he pushed. The house was old and the door uneven, so he'd been opening it that way for a long time. He'd planned to have it fixed before leaving for Japan, but he'd been in too much of a rush. It tugged at his heartstrings a little to see that the door was still uneven.

The old door rattled, and Haruko's heart jumped.

Behind the door was a small room with a yellow linoleum floor. The walls were lined with framed pictures. As her eyes roved around nervously, Haruko noticed that Jonghyeok was in a lot of them.

To one side was the kitchen with an old cupboard, piled with bowls and dishes. Like an old movie, there was a water pump, and a ladle made of a real gourd was floating on the water inside the jar.

On the dirt floor between the kitchen and the room was a pair of old, stretched-out rubber shoes. A basket lay on the warm stone floor, alongside partially dealt *hwatu* cards. Next to the small floor table that his grandmother had put aside with a sheet of newspaper over the dishes was a box of drinks in fancy wrapping paper that seemed out of place in a house like this and had obviously been left by the people outside.

At the sound of the door opening, an old lady's voice pierced through the air.

"I don't want to do it! Go away! Get out!"

Jonghyeok's grandmother was lying curled on her side like a curved ox horn with her head on a wooden pillow in the warmest area of her small *ondol* room. Cats sat crouched around as if protecting her. Grandma didn't move an inch and continued to yell without even looking. Her sharp voice rang high.

"What do you want me to say? I have nothing to say to you. Just get out! Out!"

Her refusal was strong.

Meow!

A black cat mewed at Jonghyeok, as if welcoming him instead of his grandmother. Taking off his shoes, Jonghyeok called to his grandmother.

"Grandma, it's me, Jonghyeok."

Grandma stopped yelling and asked, "Who? Who is it?"

"Grandma, it's Jonghyeok. Your grandson's home."

At his words, she slowly sat up. One of the cats that had been crouching on top of her slid to the floor. Through the strands of white hair that fell disheveled down to her eyes, the old woman squinted at the person in front of her. Her small face with a toothless mouth formed even more wrinkles.

"Oh dear, you're Jonghyeok! You're here! My grandson Jonghyeok's home!"

Grandma flung out her arms to embrace him. She was too small and thin to hold her grown-up grandson. Jonghyeok held her instead in a warm embrace. As if she couldn't believe her eyes, she held Jonghyeok's face in her hands and beheld him with their foreheads touching.

"You're Jonghyeok. You're really my grandson Jonghyeok. I saw a golden orb-weaver come down from the ceiling today and heard a magpie chatter loudly in the quiet morning. They must have been here to tell me that you were coming! My boy…"

As she examined Jonghyeok's face, her gaze was full of love and her voice was full of warmth. Only after her emotions had settled down did she notice Haruko, who was still standing on the dirt floor by the entrance to the room.

"Who's the girl standing outside the room over there?"

Jonghyeok introduced her to his grandmother. "She's a

friend studying at the same university as me, Grandma."

"Oh dear, an important guest!" Grandma said, as she pulled herself closer toward the door and held out her hand toward Haruko. "Come on up here."

"Hello, Grandmother." Haruko grabbed Grandma's hand and bowed. Grandma held Haruko's hand and stroked it, asking, "You must have come from Seoul, then? That's a long way. How great!"

Grandma held Jonghyeok's hand and Haruko's again, thankful that the two of them had come to see her.

"Some strange people came to visit today, but my precious grandson came too!"

A smile spread across Grandma's face, and Haruko looked at her closely. The old woman was wearing a *jeogori* top made of old silk. She must have had it for a long time because the sleeves were frayed and tattered. Her clothes were old, but they were clean as if freshly washed.

White hair like snow covered the top of her head; her face was wrinkled like a withered napa cabbage leaf; her back was hunched over like a clamp; and her toothless, puckered face was dotted with liver spots. Yet her gaze was bright and alive, like that of a ferocious animal living deep in the mountains.

Jonghyeok took out the various clothes and health products he'd bought for his grandmother. And then he took out a carton of cigarettes. He opened a pack and pushed one end of a cigarette out for her.

Grandma took it without hesitation and stuck it between her lips. Jonghyeok looked for a lighter but couldn't find one.

"Do you have a lighter?" Jonghyeok asked.

Grandma fumbled around the floor and produced a matchbox. Haruko looked with interest at the small box made with glue and paper as Grandma handed it to her. She lit a match and held it up to Grandma's cigarette.

Grandma inhaled the smoke deeply and said, "It tastes good. Very clean." Then she turned and asked Jonghyeok, "This wasn't made in Japan, was it?"

Jonghyeok answered, "No, Grandma. No way. I bought it in Yanji before I came here. It's made in China."

Haruko felt a pang of guilt for no reason. She picked up the ashtray and held it for Grandma to tap off the ashes. Watching her, Grandma asked, "So, what's your name?"

Flustered and at a loss for words, Haruko looked at

Jonghyeok, who also panicked. He'd planned to deceive his grandmother but hadn't thought of a Korean name for Haruko beforehand.

"It's… Chunhwa," Jonghyeok made up a name, using the first Chinese character in Haruko's real name.

"Chunhwa?" Grandma repeated. "Oh dear, that's very similar to my name."

"Pardon?" asked Haruko.

"My name's Chunja."

"Really?"

Haruko looked at Jonghyeok in surprise. She then remembered how he'd often said she had the same name as someone else he knew. Sitting in her presence, Haruko felt as if she were dreaming.

"You're still a flower, Grandma," said Jonghyeok charmingly as he scooted closer to her.

"Me? A flower? Where in the world have you seen such an old flower?" Grandma laughed, covering her puckered mouth with a hand as gnarled as tree bark.

"You're a granny flower. Have you seen how pretty those granny flowers are?"

"Oh, my baby."

Pleased at his words, she patted his bottom as though

he were a child.

"How are the cats, Grandma?" asked Jonghyeok as he looked lovingly at the cats in the room. He picked up the one crouching against Grandma, held it in his arms, and stroked it.

"Good, good. All the cats are as healthy as I am."

When the conversation landed on cats, the corners of Grandma's puckered mouth turned up, and a smile spread across her face.

"All six of them are here." She recited their names out loud as she pointed at each one. "Over there's Sunhwa, Gwang-ok, Okbun, Yeongsin, Hye-ok, and Malja."

"Oh, all the *neko* have names," said Haruko with surprise, before realizing that she'd said "cats" in Japanese. Nervously, she glanced over at Jonghyeok. Thankfully, Grandma's hearing wasn't all that good, and she hadn't heard.

Haruko took one of the cats into her arms. She stroked its head to hide her nervousness.

Grandmother and grandson were happily chatting in the warm corner of the room when the door opened and the people who had been standing outside entered the house.

In a polite yet friendly manner, they bowed to Grandma and said, "Ma'am, we're sorry to bother you again."

While they talked with Grandma, Jonghyeok came outside and called his mother to one corner of the yard by the straw fence.

The spring weather was fickle in the countryside. Jonghyeok had taken off his jacket when he landed at the airport because the weather was so hot it nearly felt like the beginning of summer. Yet now he found himself enveloped by a breeze carrying an eerie chill. The hazy spring sunlight falling on the alley behind Grandma's house and even the newly sprouting buds on the apricot tree in one corner of the yard seemed to have turned pale.

Zipping up his jacket all the way to his neck, Jonghyeok asked his mother what was going on.

"I tipped them off," said his mother, with her hand on the fence.

"Tipped them off about what? Grandma?"

She nodded. For a moment, Jonghyeok felt faint.

"Are you sure? She really was… one?"

He couldn't bear to say the word "comfort woman."

73

Instead of a verbal answer, his mother nodded again. It was a firm and resolute nod. Jonghyeok felt like there was a flock of white birds inside his head, spreading their wings to take flight. It was now his turn to steady himself with a hand on the fence, as he felt his knees might give in.

"Then you knew everything?" Jonghyeok asked. "About how Grandma was… one of them?"

His mother nodded again. Jonghyeok shook his head in disbelief. A look of incredulity crossed his features. He'd seen and heard the news about comfort women on television and in newspapers, but he'd never imagined it would affect his life in any way. He certainly had never thought his own grandmother might be one—he still couldn't. The end of a sorghum stalk broke off in his hand from the fence.

His mother took off her glasses and dabbed her eyes with her hand. With a tearful face, she said, "It was a painful decision. It hurts, but we have to let the world know. About your grandmother and her story."

She enunciated every word. Her resolute face was the one she'd often worn as a leader of the women's movement.

"And I trust that a doctoral candidate like yourself would know that this is the right thing to do. You know what the Japanese are doing these days and that we all have the responsibility to uncover the truth about their crimes against the comfort women."

As she spoke those words, Jonghyeok noticed her chapped lips. It seemed that she'd been worried sick about this.

"But how…" Jonghyeok rubbed his wind-beaten face with both his hands. He simply couldn't accept the connection between his grandmother and the two words "comfort woman."

"I'd once read an article that there were 200,000 comfort women in China," his mother began in a low but strong voice. "That means there are 200,000 painful stories similar to your grandma's. But I also saw on the news about how only a few dozen are still alive. Your grandmother's one of them.

"She's over ninety, and knowing all the pain and difficulties she experienced, I wanted to let her live out the rest of her life quietly in peace. But… we need to tell the world the truth. If we don't step up, then that history, that pain, will remain buried forever in the dark. Don't you agree?"

His mother gazed at Jonghyeok through her glasses.

"You have to be part of this. We're doing this for her. So lend an ear to the painful story of your grandmother. She loves you to death."

Jonghyeok tilted his head back and stared at the sky. He was heartbroken. Tears began to well up in his eyes. His mother took off her glasses again to wipe her tears. Then she held her hand up to Jonghyeok's face to wipe the tears from the corners of his eyes.

He felt someone stir from behind. He hadn't been aware, but Haruko was standing behind him. There was something like terror in her eyes as she watched Jonghyeok and his mother.

When Jonghyeok entered Grandma's room again, she was surrounded by a mass of people. She gestured at him to come closer as though he were her savior. Jonghyeok rushed to her side. He sat close beside her and held her hand. Her hand was warm. It was also trembling. Jonghyeok stroked her clenched fist and massaged the leg that had been injured in the car accident.

A laptop sat open on the floor. The power cord

stretched across the stove and plugged into an outlet in the kitchen. Some people were watching a video playing on the laptop.

On the screen, Jonghyeok could see a crowd of people in front of a building in the rain. Soon there was a close-up of the sign on the building: "Embassy of Japan." There were old ladies with gray hair wearing masks on their faces. People in the front were holding a huge banner that said, "Wednesday Demonstration Demanding Japan Redress the Comfort Women Issue." Heavy rain pelted the banner. Protesters were holding picket signs with different messages. The camera zoomed in on some of them.

"No peace without justice!"

"Truth will be remembered!"

"You must admit your guilt!"

The protesters were shouting slogans in the rain. The old ladies repeated after them.

"Let's restore the respect and rights to the comfort women!"

"The Japanese government must admit that the comfort women system was a crime committed as State policy!"

"The Japanese government must apologize to the victims!"

"Apologize! Apologize!"

The loud shouts burst out of the speakers on the laptop. Grandma sat, watching the people shouting the slogans in the rain, the tear-softened corners of her eyes trembling.

"Twenty-three years," the coalition's team leader spoke in a loud voice for Jonghyeok's grandmother, who had poor hearing. "For twenty-three years, these women who have the same painful stories as yours have been fighting the Japanese."

In a clear, passionate voice, she explained the story of the old ladies who had been protesting about the comfort women issue in front of the Japanese embassy every Wednesday for the past twenty-three years.

"The first demonstration was held on a Wednesday in January 1992. Since then, these demonstrations have been held without fail every Wednesday at noon in front of the Japanese embassy in Seoul. More than a thousand demonstrations have been held so far, and even teenagers and foreigners are taking part. On special days, such as International Women's Day, the demonstrations are held across the globe—not only in Korea but also in the United

States, France, the Philippines, and the Netherlands!"

She spoke without a pause. Jonghyeok noticed indescribably deep fatigue on her face and on the faces of those around her. But pushing through the tiredness, the team leader continued her speech.

"We need your help in bringing your story to other people to prevent such a painful and wrongful history from repeating itself. Please."

Grandma cast a glance at Jonghyeok. Realizing what she wanted, he took a cigarette out of a pack and placed it between her lips. He struck a match and lit the cigarette for her. She inhaled deep, filling her lungs with smoke. Then she let out a stream of white smoke with a sigh.

After quickly finishing the cigarette, with her eyes glued to the laptop screen, Grandma reached her hand out to Jonghyeok again.

But he shook his head, "No more today, Grandma. You smoked a lot already."

"Just give me one more," she insisted, holding out her hand.

Reluctantly, Jonghyeok lit another one for her. The house was thick with smoke.

When the video ended, the team leader took

something out and handed it to Grandma. It was a photograph of a painting. An oil painting of a girl with big eyes. In the painting, the girl was wearing a white *jeogori* top and a black skirt. She was being led somewhere by a man in a tan uniform. A big hand was grasping the girl's wrist like a handcuff. The girl's eyes were wide with fear. On the ground next to the girl, balloon flowers blossomed piteously.

"This was painted by one of the old ladies who had been a comfort woman," explained the team leader as she held up the painting.

"Jonghyeok, bring me my eyes," said Grandma, who had not spoken a word to the people who'd reentered her house or even glanced at them.

Haruko's loving gaze followed Jonghyeok as he headed to the kitchen and opened a drawer in the center of the cupboard. From the glasses case inside, he took out a pair of spectacles. He knew exactly where everything was in Grandma's house, which showed how much he loved his grandmother. Watching him, Haruko's eyes filled with warmth.

Jonghyeok wiped the lenses with the end of his sleeve and placed the glasses on his grandmother's face.

Through the glasses, Grandma examined the painting.

"She painted what happened when she was taken by Japanese soldiers," the team leader explained. "The lady who painted this is Kim Sun-deok. She was taken by the Japanese soldiers from Gyeongsangnam-do in Korea to Shanghai, where she suffered all sorts of hardship."

Grandma carefully scrutinized the painting with interest.

The team leader continued, "Ms. Kim made paintings like this to let the world know about the crimes committed by the Japanese people until she passed away ten years ago."

Grandma's shoulders twitched. She held the painting in her hands and looked at it from up close, almost touching it to her face. She kept on staring at the painting right in front of her face. The photograph trembled like an iris fluttering in the wind.

Then a strange sound escaped from her throat. It sounded like dammed-up water trying to flow out through a narrow sluice gate. It was a moan. Her moans soon turned into rippling sobs that grew as loud as the surge and then as loud as the waves.

Eventually, Grandma began to wail. She sat crumpled

on the floor and cried out loud. Tears poured down her cheeks, and snot and saliva flowed down her face as she wept miserably. Without even thinking to cover her face, she cried and wailed.

"Here's a handkerchief, ma'am," said one of the coalition members, handing it to her. Embarrassed, Haruko also took out her handkerchief. She didn't understand everything, but a strange pain welled up inside her heart and tears fogged up her eyes as she watched Jonghyeok's grandmother crying her heart out.

"Let her be," said Jonghyeok's mother. "Perhaps crying will help her get some of her sorrow off her chest."

Grandma fell into Jonghyeok's arms. Burying her face in his lap, she wept and wailed at the top of her lungs. The sound of her cries reverberated through his body.

Jonghyeok wiped the tears and the saliva dripping from her mouth with his hands. But no matter how much he wiped her face, the tears kept on coming like water gushing from a backed-up gutter.

It was a wail of bitter grief.

The sound of her cries mingled with the early spring wind that brushed against the paper doors and rang through the old house for a long time.

Grandma sat down cross-legged again in the warm corner of the room. She was wearing the dentures that she never wore because they were too cumbersome. Her dry, brittle white hair was neatly combed back and held in a knot by a copper spoon instead of a hairpin. She asked for her ashtray to be emptied, and once it was, she put it on her lap.

Then she said, "I'd like to ask some of you to leave."

She pointed to some of the people in the room, first of whom was the cameraman, setting up a tripod.

She said, "I'd like all the men to leave."

The cameraman knitted his brows and said, "We have to film the interview, ma'am."

"Then I won't talk."

She put her foot down. Her voice was unexpectedly firm.

"Go on out," the team leader nudged the cameraman toward the door. "I can shoot the interview."

A male editor also left the room at Grandma's insistence.

"You go, too," she said to Jonghyeok.

"I want to stay, Grandma," replied Jonghyeok, playing on her affection. "Let me stay by your side."

"Go. Go, now."

Jonghyeok lingered, not eager to get up.

"Wouldn't it be okay for him to stay?" the team leader asked. "He's your grandson after all."

Grandma snapped her head up and responded in a cold voice.

"You want an old lady to tell a painful story that'll strip her naked in front of her own grandson?" she screeched in a steely voice that made people's hair stand on end. It sounded like broken pottery shards rubbing against each other. It was also loud, and Jonghyeok's mother quickly shook her head at him, signaling to exit the room.

Reluctantly, Jonghyeok stood up. When Haruko got up with him, Grandma grabbed her hand.

"You stay. No need to go."

Haruko was taken aback. Not knowing what to do, she looked at Jonghyeok, pleading for him to step in. It was his first visit to his hometown in years, but he looked grave, as if enveloped in a black shroud.

I wanted to show Haruko my cozy little hometown and my kind, healthy grandmother, Jonghyeok thought. *But now...*

Haruko knew exactly what he was thinking. He was

acting indifferently, but his eyes were constantly wavering with anxiety, and Haruko could read his embarrassment. Jonghyeok strained to curl the corners of his mouth into a smile as he looked at Haruko and nodded.

Grandma asked for another cigarette. Haruko pulled one out of the pack and put it between Grandma's lips. She picked up the matchbox and struck a match. She must have been nervous because she couldn't light it. She tried again but failed again. Grandma took the match from Haruko and struck it. A small flame came to life.

After lighting the cigarette in her mouth, Grandma inhaled deeply. Not knowing what to do next, Haruko sat back down next to her and shyly lowered her head. Tiny motes of dust were floating in the air as rays of morning sunlight streamed through the window, which was still covered with last winter's sheet of plastic insulation. In the sunlight, Grandma sat like a dry mummy freshly awoken after thousands of years.

As the sunlight grew stronger, Haruko noticed all the small wrinkles like constellations on Grandma's face, as sallow as bleached muslin. Deep in thought, Grandma knitted her faint eyebrows. Under them, her pupils seemed perpetually empty or completely full.

As the sunlight sluggishly brightened the room, an uncomfortable silence hung heavy in the air. Everyone waited, holding their breath and staring at Grandma's puckered and wrinkly mouth, which remained tightly closed.

Grandma didn't utter a single word for several hours. She was having a difficult time digging up the traces of that dreadfully sickening, horrifying nightmare from her memory.

Hoot!

The call of a scops owl rang clearly outside the window. As if taking a cue from the bird, Grandma put out the cigarette, which had burned down to the stub, in the ashtray. Then she pushed the ashtray to one side.

Finally, she opened her trembling mouth. The cigarette smoke she'd inhaled deep into her lungs curled out from the corners of her lips. And with the smoke, Grandma began the story that had sunk so deep in her heart with the emotions that had been bottled up for so long.

"I was born with an absurdly wretched fate. It was like water from ten trenches was all flowing into my one trench. It was a terrible, miserable fate. On the day I was born, Walbon people invaded my hometown of Deer

Valley. It was a day when fires and floods happened on the same day."

"Walbon?" asked the team leader, who had been jotting things down in her notebook. "Do you mean Ilbon (Japan)?"

"Right, Walbon people," Grandma repeated.

A cat mewed quietly by her side. Grandma stopped talking and looked down at the cats.

"Come here, Gwang-ok and Yeongsin," she called to them. After setting down the white one by her lap, she held the black one in her arms. Stroking its back, she began to tell her story.

"It was the spring of 1920, when azaleas began to bloom on the hills nearby . . ."

A Tragedy in Deer Valley

Kkeutsun was running for her life.

She pushed through the silver grass lashing at her calves and splashed through the stream that came up to her ankles. Every time she tripped over a rock and fell, she immediately picked herself up to run and run again. The train of her long skirt got caught on the branch of a birch tree. Hurriedly, she yanked at it, and it tore. She ran again, with the tattered train of her skirt blowing in the wind. The piece of torn cloth left behind on a tree stump flapped pathetically.

Bunching the cloth of her cumbersome skirt in front of her, Kkeutsun ran and ran. Her mouth twitched, ready to burst into a cry at any moment, even as she kept on running.

It was a truly strange sight. Not because she was

running as fast as she could with all her might. It was because she was in the last month of pregnancy. It was surprising how fast she was moving, holding her huge belly. Had anyone been watching, they might have worried that she would hurt herself and the baby.

As she struggled to run as fast as she could, a sharp shout rang out from behind her. More shouts followed like strong tentacles, trying to latch onto her.

"*Tomare* (Halt)!"

"*Tomare* (Stop)! *Soko ni tomarankai* (Stop right there)!"

Like a pack of wild dogs, the pursuers shouted at her with harsh voices like nails scratching a chalkboard. A group of men were chasing after her. They were all in military uniform. In their hands were rifles with bayonets. Their shouts lashed out at her like whips, mercilessly striking her ears and back, but even as the shouts flogged her she ran.

Kkeutsun didn't understand what they were shouting. Her pursuers were shouting in Japanese. She thought perhaps everything that had happened today was just a nightmare. The most frightfully dreadful one she'd ever dreamed in her life. A nightmare that she never wanted to have again.

Even as she ran, she thought she must be dreaming a terrible dream that no one would wake her from. A frightening night terror. It was better to think that way.

As she kept on running, she thought about all the nightmares she'd had. The day she had been chased by a black dog owned by a Chinese family across the river, Kkeutsun had a nightmare. A monster with a face that was all teeth kept on chasing her. Those large pointy teeth seemed ready to crush her bones. Someone had shaken her awake as she moaned breathlessly in her nightmare.

She also remembered the nightmare she had on the winter's night when she'd dropped and broken the water jar and nearly fallen into the well. In that dream, she was falling down, down into a bottomless abyss. She'd screamed so loud in her sleep that her father awoke with a start and kicked her hard in her buttocks. Only then was she able to rouse from that terrible scene.

But what was happening now was a much more horrendous dream compared to those. It was a combination of all the nightmares—a huge monster with large, pointy teeth was doggedly chasing her, and someone had booted her down into the well, and there were more monsters with large, pointy teeth waiting for her at the bottom of the abyss.

This nightmare of a tragedy began by a well in the morning. A woman, known as the "Well Lady" because her house was located near the well in the outskirts of the village, headed to the well early in the morning and stopped short as if she'd been doused with a bucket of cold water. There was already a crowd of people gathered there. There were so many of them that the Well Lady turned pale at the strangely alarming and fearsome sight.

Each and every one of them was clad in brownish-yellow uniform, wearing a military cap, and sitting atop a black horse. All of them had long rifles slung on their backs.

The man who seemed to be the leader tugged on the reins, and his horse stepped out toward the Well Lady. The red band around the edge of his peaked cap and the red insignia on the collar of his uniform offended the eyes. There were three yellow stars on the insignia. He was wearing a belt with a long sword in a sheath and holding a riding crop in his hand. Glaring at the Well Lady with sunken eyes, he waved the crop in his hand.

Several men dismounted and dragged another man down from a horse. He was bound with a rope. It was clear that he'd been beaten. His eyes were blue from bruises, and the corners of his lips were torn. There was dried blood on his mouth. His white clothes were also spotted with blood seeping through.

The uniformed men pushed him toward the Well Lady. Appearing delirious from severe beatings, the man gazed blankly at her with unfocused, hollow eyes. One of the soldiers swung the stock of his rifle and mercilessly struck the man's shoulder. He staggered and barely managed to part his dry lips. A faint voice that seemed to be coming from the underworld escaped his lips as he asked, "Whe… where is Ryang's house?"

The Well Lady was too stunned to talk.

The man smacked his dry lips once and struggled to ask again, "Yeongsin School Principal Ryang. His house."

Only then did the Well Lady come to her senses and held out her arm to point to a house by the entrance of the village. Her finger trembled like the sleeve of a shirt on a scarecrow fluttering in the autumn wind.

A horse snorted, and Red Insignia held up his crop and pointed its tip forward.

The group of soldiers began to shift. An array of cavalrymen left the dazed Well Lady and headed into the village, pushing the beaten man to lead the group. Right then, the prisoner started running toward the village. Still bound by a rope, he began to yell as he ran. Barely squeezing out a hoarse voice from his throat as if wringing a washcloth, he roared, "Run! The Japanese are here! Just ru..."

He didn't finish his last sentence. Red Insignia had rushed his horse after the man, and the sharp edge of his murderous sword cut through the air. The man's severed head flew through the air before it fell and rolled on the ground like a pumpkin. His headless body took a couple of steps forward and tumbled down to the ground. The horses trampled the headless body as the cavalrymen barged into the village.

Shoved by the stock of the rifle and prodded by bayonets, the villagers gathered in the schoolyard. It was a small yard where field days were held in the spring, as well as small and big village events throughout the year. In preparation for the field day that was scheduled to be held soon, there was a tall wooden gateway made out of pine branches in the yard. Winners of various events at the field day would receive plaques and prizes in front of this wooden gateway.

The schoolyard that had been aflutter with excitement was frozen over with cold tension. Overbearing soldiers in brownish-yellow uniforms and flashing swords wore hard-set expressions as though they were facing their biggest enemies. The bayonets on the muzzles of the rifles glistened in the morning sunlight. Scared into submission, the people stood cowering and barely moving.

Kkeutsun stood close by her husband. He grasped her nervous hand in his. With a face sallow from illness, he looked at her with concern. Kkeutsun's husband was a teacher at Yeongsin School. A graduate of Daeseong Middle School in Longjing, he taught Korean history. For an uneducated woman who had been past her marriageable years like Kkeutsun, marrying a school teacher from a big town was enough to arouse jealousy from other women in the village. It was all thanks to her father, who was a terribly reserved man but of good moral character.

The villagers paid teachers with money they earned from portions of their fields. Despite financial struggles, Kkeutsun's father paid the most. And at the time, her future husband came to eat most frequently at their house and ended up staying there permanently. His only possible weakness was that he was in frail health. He always had a grubby blanket covering his lap and sat in the warmest corner of the room, coughing up a fit. Small medicine pouches usually hung like drying garlic along the crossbeam.

Kkeutsun thought the world of her husband, and the two were a loving couple who were about to see the fruition of their love.

The villagers cast glances toward the edge of the schoolyard, where a willow tree was standing. The tree had been planted in an empty lot by the first people who moved and settled down in the village. The school now sat in that empty lot. The willow tree had been something of a sacred village tree, but when their eyes rested on it now, fear seized the onlookers.

There was a man hanging from the tree. It was Principal Ryang. Like a moth stuck to a strong spiderweb, he was hung high up on a branch by his torso, his legs squirming and swinging in the air. The edges of his clothes fluttered in the wind.

He was the school principal and a village elder. He

oversaw big and small events in the village and turned his school in this remote village in the mountains into one where even Korean-Russian students came to learn. He also had connections with the anti-Japanese Righteous Army in northern Jiandao, who often visited Deer Valley. The Japanese soldiers had tied up such a man of virtue and hung him on a tree like an animal about to be slaughtered.

Yet even as he was tied up, Principal Ryang held his head high.

Red Insignia had one hand on his waist and the other on the hilt of the sword on his belt. Without a word, he glared at the villagers with his hollow eyes, capturing their faces in his memory as if taking pictures. The sword that had recently drawn human blood hung by his waist. Red Insignia's round pupils were clear and tight, ready to seize anyone in front of him by the throat. Terrified by his menacing glare, people dropped their heads every time his gaze landed on them.

Red Insignia held up his crop and flicked his wrist. A short and stocky soldier stepped up in front of the people. Like a man straining to pass a hard stool, he scrunched up his face in a frown, raised his chin, and began to yell at the top of his lungs.

"People of Deer Valley! Listen up! This here is Captain Suzuki of the 14th Army Division, who oversees this region."

Red Insignia, who was referred to as Suzuki, gave a slight nod to the people. The stocky soldier continued without even taking a breath. His Korean was decent although a bit halting.

"Captain Suzuki wishes to speak to the people of Deer Valley about the reason we came to the village."

The captain came forward and began to speak slowly, tapping his palm with the tip of the crop. His voice was razor-sharp.

"From now on, you must *kyoujo* (cooperate) with us without question. We have come to this *buraku* (village) on patrol to seek out *futeisenjin* (rebellious Koreans) with subversive ideas about the Great Empire of Japan."

The stocky soldier repeated the captain's words in Korean. Suddenly, Suzuki's voice rose an octave into a shrill bark.

"To our regret, we acquired information that all the people of this *buraku* are *futeisenjin*, fighting against the Great Empire of Japan."

The captain's face reddened like a hot stove. His voice was stiff with rage, and the words seemed to come out by fits and starts.

"Today! We are here to take care of your leaders *sokkoku* (at once)!"

The captain shot daggers toward the willow tree. His sunken eyes seemed to be glinting with something like a blue phosphorescent light emerging from the stump of a tree that had been struck by lightning. With a scarlet face, he drew his sword from its sheath.

The soldiers formed a single horizontal line and loaded their rifles—*clack, clack, clack, clack*. The muzzles of the rifles were raised. The black holes were aimed at the willow tree, at Principal Ryang.

The corpulent captain stepped forward and shouted, "*Youi* (Ready)!"

His cutthroat voice rang out again, "*Hatsha* (Shoot)!"

Crack! Crack! Crack! Crack! Violent gunshots resonated, shaking up the quiet and peaceful Deer Valley. At the ear-piercing sound of gunshots, children began to cry and dogs barked. Willow tree leaves tore from the branches and flew through the air. The barrage of bullets shredded the body of Principal Ryang, tied up and hanging on the tree.

A startled scream erupted from the crowd.

A woman ran toward the willow tree, wailing, "Darling!"

"Father!" a young man cried out, following after the woman.

Crack! Crack! Two more shots tore through the air, and Principal Ryang's wife and son fell in front of the willow tree.

At the tragedy that took place in front of their eyes in an instant, the villagers were stunned. Everyone stood rooted to the ground with a dazed look on their faces.

There was a reason the Japanese regarded Principal Ryang as an enemy. Throngs of people continued to cross the rivers into China from Korea to avoid Japan's intensifying colonial policy. Many refugees and anti-Japanese fighters left their homes and escaped to Deer Valley, and unbeknownst to most people, the village was turning into the center of operations for the anti-Japanese movement.

In the anti-Japanese protest that rocked the entire city of Longjing last spring, the people of Deer Valley had been there without fail. Kkeutsun had also witnessed the spectacle in Longjing with her own eyes. She'd followed her husband even though he tried to discourage her. It was her first visit to Longjing, and she was excited, full of simple curiosity and expectations about going to a big city.

On that day, the people of Deer Valley and the teachers and students of Yeongsin School bundled up the rice balls they'd made the previous evening and traveled miles in the early morning to Longjing. The city streets were full of agitated crowds and overflowing with tension.

People were gathering in small groups in the Ruidian meadow in Longjing. Men in traditional white *durumagi* overcoats and women in *jeogori* tops, as well as white-haired old men and women and small children rallied like dark clouds gathering on a rainy day. Like tributaries flowing into the river, people from various parts of northern Jiandao poured into Longjing, the "Seoul of Jiandao" and the fulcrum of Korean people's will for independence.

The protest was held in an ordinary schoolyard. In the center of the yard, flags hung high up on the poles with the words "Justice and Humanity" and "Hurrah for Korean Independence!" The belfry of a church stood tall near the yard. Kkeutsun narrowed her eyes and saw that the belfry was full of small children, trying to get a good look at the spectacle unfolding below.

Ding! Ding! The bell tolled, sending its echoes through the sky above the Ruidian meadow.

"We Koreans proclaim liberation. We proclaim our sovereignty! We proclaim justice! We proclaim humanitarianism!

"We are a people with a glorious history, we are a people of diligence. Yet there are people who aim to break us and destroy us. … The tears of patriots filled the sea and the people's bitter cries reached the sky. The heavens heard our voices, and the heavens turned to us. Now that the luck of the times has shifted and the country has changed, the bells of justice ring throughout the streets and the ship of liberty has reached the port.

"We are one of the nations under heaven. We are one of the oppressed. Today, in obedience to heavens and in response to the people's demands, tens of millions of people are marching on equal grounds, singing songs of freedom in unison with our hands balled up into fists. Claiming to be the leader of Eastern Civilization and the bastion of peace in the East, Japan has invaded us and altered the current political landscape. ...

"We shall join together in one mind and with one purpose to stop the invaders from trampling on Jiandao. Everyone has this sacred responsibility, and therefore the 800,000 Koreans in Jiandao shall use all our strength for the equality of humanity even if we are headed for the underworld."

Once the proclamation was fully recited, thunderous roars of *manseh* (Korean for "hurrah") shook the sky and the earth. People who had moved to Jiandao to avoid Japanese oppression opened their eyes to their historical calling and went on shouting *manseh* at the top of their lungs. The shouts echoed around the Hailian riverside for a long time.

Shouting *manseh*, the protesters began to march. Led by her husband, Kkeutsun joined the marching crowd. People filled the streets such that it was impossible to see either end of the mass of humanity. At the very front of the protesters was a flagbearer, holding a flag that read "We support Korean Independence." The "Loyal Devotion Group" consisting of about three hundred teachers and students from various schools in the region led the crowd of people who had gathered from near and far.

"*Manseh* for Korean independence!"

"We oppose Japan's invasion!"

"Down with pro-Japanese lackeys!"

Shouting the slogans at the top of their lungs, protesters proudly marched toward the Japanese Consulate General, located in the center of Longjing.

A sudden commotion broke out in the front. Near the consulate building, a fight had broken out between the protesters and the soldiers and police who were trying to stop the crowd. Outraged, people kept on pushing forward, throwing rocks at the soldiers and policemen, who were frightened by the crowd's urgency and determination.

Crack! A gunshot rang out. The flagbearer who had been standing with a flag at the front of the crowd fell down. Agitated by the disturbance, the Chinese police who had been abetted by their Japanese counterparts opened fire on the protesters. More gunshots followed like the sound of popping corn, and people in the frontlines began to fall one by one. Unarmed protesters began to scatter from the scene of carnage.

Kkeutsun didn't remember how her husband led her away from the chaos in Longjing. Later, she heard from

Principal Ryang that over ten people were killed by the Japanese soldiers and policemen on that day and over twenty were injured.

This was why the Japanese came to regard Deer Valley as the center of "rebellious activity," and they'd been watching for an opportunity to raid the village.

The moment they saw the principal bleeding and dying in front of their eyes, the villagers began to tremble, trapped in fear. Terror pressed down on Kkeutsun like a huge boulder. Enveloped by panic that made her hair stand on end, she hunched her shoulders and held her round belly as if to protect her unborn baby.

Suzuki shouted toward the people, who were shaking with fear. The stocky soldier translated, using a mix of Japanese words and Korean.

"*Jyoshi* (women), stay where you are, and adult *danshi* (men), step forward. *Hayaku* (quickly)!"

Hesitantly men stepped forward out of the crowd. Japanese soldiers viciously struck the men on their backs with the stocks of their rifles. One soldier noticed a man standing crouched behind the women and dragged him out by the collar. He struck the man's cheek with his horsewhip. A bloody line formed across his face. The soldier grabbed the man by his hair and dragged him away.

Kkeutsun's father was also being taken away. Her reserved father stayed silent as usual as he was taken away. Kkeutsun's husband was dragged away as well. While being taken away, her husband turned around. With a face as yellow as a crown daisy, he stared at Kkeutsun. His gaze was full of concern for her, in the final month of pregnancy. Feeling his caring gaze on her, Kkeutsun felt the corners of her eyes twitch as tears welled up. Hesitantly, her husband kept on turning around and looking back at her, and the soldier taking him ruthlessly booted him in the back.

About thirty men of the village were all rounded up and taken into the school building with a single classroom, leaving all the women in the schoolyard. Having no idea what the Japanese were planning, the women simply watched with fear in their eyes.

The soldiers closed the door to the school and locked it. The women thought that they were simply locking the men in the school when several soldiers began to break down the wooden gate that had been set up in the yard.

They took the broken pine branches and boards and piled them up around the school building. They also brought the firewood that the villagers had cut and neatly stacked up in their yards, piling that up as well. They broke off more branches from oak and pine trees, and even brought millet straw bales.

It wasn't at all clear to the women what the soldiers were doing, but their actions seemed alarming. The women's hearts began to pound in fear.

Some of the soldiers came running with dark green cans. They unscrewed the caps and started pouring the contents onto the piles of wood around the school. A strong smell of gasoline hit the women's noses.

The women's eyes wavered with apprehension, and their hearts pounded even faster. One of them started sobbing, calling out for her husband. Red Insignia snapped his head around and glowered. The cry quickly subsided.

Having finished the preparations, the soldiers once again stood in a line. They loaded their rifles—*clack, clack, clack, clack.* Kkeutsun started at the noise. The muzzles were up in the air. They were aimed at the window of the school building.

One soldier held a makeshift torch made out of a broken pine branch with one end covered in sap. He lit the torch and threw it onto the woodpile. It caught fire in an instant. The dry pine tree branches and timber soaked in gasoline were extremely flammable, and the school building—built of wooden posts and plastered walls fastened together with straw rope—was enveloped in flames within seconds.

The women who had stood befuddled screamed all at once.

Black smoke spilled out into the sky uncontrollably, and the flames leapt out of the window, tips licking the walls. The blazing fire climbed up to the door posts with smoke and its red tongue began to lick the eaves of the roof. Coughing and screaming, the men broke the only window with their bare fists. With their hair and clothes aflame, the men started climbing out the window.

Crack! Crack! The Japanese soldiers fired without pity at the men who were trying to escape the school. They swung their swords and plunged their bayonets into those who had rushed through the smoke and were painfully coughing. With light strokes, they severed the men's heads so easily, like a knife slicing through tofu. Within moments, heads rolled in the schoolyard like balls.

Gunshots blasted throughout the school grounds and Deer Valley. Writhing in smoke and flames, some of the men poked their heads out of the window and were killed, their torsos hanging out of the building. The Well Lady's husband jumped out of the window and started running, but bullets soon pierced his back, and he dropped to the ground with blood in his mouth. Deacon Heo poked his head out of the smoke, only to have it blasted into pieces like a watermelon. Hunter Choe ran out of the building but tripped over a corpse after only a few steps. A soldier rushed over to him right away and plunged his bayonet into his back. With his body covered in stab and bullet wounds, Choe picked himself up with all the strength left in him. He reached out his hand into the air as if to grasp something and collapsed.

Screaming in her high-pitched voice, the Well Lady started running toward the burning school. One soldier grabbed her shoulder and pulled her back. She jerked herself loose from his grasp and tried to run again. Then the soldier stabbed her in the back with his bayonet. The sharp blade sank into her body as if it were pumpkin and slid back out, covered in red. Blood sprayed like a fountain from her back. Without even a scream, she died.

Hunter Choe's daughter had also rushed out after the Well Lady, and she too fell when a sword struck her shoulder. Hoeryeong Lady ran out flailing her arms and lost one when a sword swung and severed it from her body. She picked up her fallen limb from the ground. Not knowing what else to do, she shrieked and screamed.

Killing people who were seized with terror was easier than snapping off dry stalks of grain. The Japanese soldiers stabbed, slashed, and hacked at the people who were struggling to save their lives.

It was a truly frightful scene. If hell were real, this would be it. The people of Deer Valley were at the mercy of inhumane devils in this eternal hell of suffering. A few of the women who were about to run to the school froze in fear. They didn't dare step forward, and only wailed, tearing at the breast-ties on their *jeogori* and digging at the ground with their feet.

"Darling!"

"Father!"

"*Oppa* (brother)!"

Amidst gut-wrenching screams and heart-breaking wails, the flames rose higher. The school building eventually crumbled, like a bird skewered with an arrow. The roof collapsed, and the flames, gray smoke, and embers soared into the sky once more.

Bitterly weeping at the atrocious murder taking place right in front of her eyes, Kkeutsun found herself wishing for something strange. She hoped that neither her father nor her husband would make it out through the window. If they did, a forest of rifles and swords was waiting for them. But if they didn't, the fires of hell were going to consume them.

This must be all a nightmare. It's just a nightmare. Kkeutsun kept on repeating these sentences in her head, holding her extended belly and panting out of fear. She was drained and paralyzed, as if she were seized by a ghost. Mixed with acrid smoke and the metallic smell of blood, drafts of air shifted with the wind at every turn that made it difficult for her to breathe.

The baby in her womb moved, as if startled. Hugging her swollen belly, Kkeutsun sank down to the ground.

No one knew when the Japanese soldiers left. People had floundered for a long time, mired in fear and despair and in the face of death. Only when the sun began to set over the Deer Rock did people realize that the carnage was over.

When the pandemonium died down and silence fell on the village, someone approached the pile of ashes and began to dig through it. The pile still held smoldering embers and heat.

When the survivors pushed aside the columns and rafters that survived the fire, they saw bodies lying about in the ashes. The corpses had been burnt black and left hunched like anchovies in the oven. It was impossible to tell who was who. Some even mistook partially burnt wood for a corpse.

Pounding their chests, the women squeezed out their tears and wails again through their hoarse throats. Weeping and crying were the only things the frail women could do. They cried, mourning the men who died such gruesome deaths and apologizing for their helplessness. All of them kept on crying, weeping, and wailing, to the point that those who hadn't witnessed what happened might think they were in a mourning competition.

In the chaos, someone burst out laughing and started running across the pile of ashes. It was Grandma Dolbae who seemed to have lost her mind at the Japanese soldiers' act of brutality. Screeching sporadically as if to chase away birds from the autumn fields, she kept on running across the pile of ashes.

Burnt black corpses were laid down in the schoolyard like dried fish. There were thirty-three bodies. All the men in the village, with the exception of Byeong-uk, who had gone to Longjing to fetch the pastor, had been slaughtered at the hands of the Japanese.

Because it was impossible to identify the bodies, the women decided to bury all the corpses together in one grave. They began to dig a huge pit by the foot of a mountain near the entrance of the village to bury the bodies all together. It took a long time for them to dig a pit large enough. Even after the sun went down, they kept on digging under the moonlight. At some point, they'd stopped crying and simply went on digging without a word. Their bodies ached with blood stasis, but they had retrieved all the bodies of their men.

Kkeutsun picked up a shovel as well. There was no one else who could do it for her now that she'd lost father and her husband. And no one was in their right mind to stop a pregnant woman from doing hard labor. As she struggled to shovel dirt from the ground, she thought hard about which of the corpses on the ground were her husband and her father. She thought she recognized one of them as her husband from his slightly bulbous head, slim stature, and his attire, but the deacon's wife said it seemed like her own husband, and even Buksan Lady said it looked like her older brother. There was no way to confirm who it was.

Holding back their tears, the women managed to bury the corpses. Sniffling and wiping their snot away, they laid the corpses in the pit one by one. They then covered them with straw mats and birch bark that they'd stripped from trees and topped it all off with dirt. A huge burial mound appeared by the hill in front of the village. Around the time they were finished piling up the dirt, it was night and rain began to fall. The misty, drizzling precipitation enveloped the village like a fog. People who had been soaked in their own tears were now damp from tears of heaven.

The mist that was neither rain nor fog brought damp moisture and flowed like tears, making people's hearts even more sodden.

When the women stood facing the grave, sorrow

swelled up in their hearts again and they threw themselves on the tomb, as if to cover its pitifulness and prevent it from getting wet. Another wave of cries and wails began. As the valley grew wet with the rain into the night, it smelled of something like cow urine. It was the stench of sorrow that had enveloped the entire valley. In the darkness covered in drizzling rain and sorrow, women who had fallen at the grave continued to wail, their cries were louder than the rain.

On that day, the Japanese soldiers had wreaked havoc in the quiet village. They set fire to the village school, church, and all the houses. The flames lasted until the next morning, and the pillar of smoke from the burning village was visible even from Longjing. All the men were massacred at the hands of the devils, and even the crowing chickens and barking dogs were slaughtered alongside them. Not a single horse, cow, chicken, or dog remained.

The next day, a woman's shrill scream rang out by the well once again. Buksan Lady had gone to the well to try and wash the bloodied and muddied clothes, but she stood shrieking with her hands grasping her head and her eyes widened.

With earthshaking hoofbeats, dozens of cavalrymen galloped toward the village once again.

Like a person traumatized by a fire going berserk at the sight of a fireplace poker, she screamed and screamed at the sight of the devilish Japanese soldiers in yellow uniforms who appeared again even before she could soothe the previous day's burning pain that had overwhelmed her like being tortured with a soldering iron. Then she fainted.

In front of the swarm of soldiers was Captain Suzuki with the three yellow stars on his red insignia. His was a face that none of the villagers ever wanted to see again.

Yelled at and prodded with the stocks of the soldiers' rifles, the women were soon gathered in front of the grave. Feeling as if the walls were closing in around them, they could barely breathe from terror. Like an angel of death, Suzuki held up his riding crop and pointed it at the grave.

"*Horikaesu* (dig it up)!"

Unable to understand him, the women looked at the captain with baffled faces.

The short and stocky soldier stepped up and spoke in inarticulate Korean, "Dig up the *haka*! Dig up the grave!"

The women were still confused. The deacon's wife asked, "The grave? You want us to dig up the grave? How come?"

The soldier's rifle stock struck her head. She fell to the ground, covering her head with her hands. Scarlet blood ran through her fingers.

"*Hayaku!*" yelled the stocky soldier, pointing at the grave.

At that moment, a loud shriek tore through the air. It was Grandma Dolbae, who was having another delirious fit. Screeching and laughing, she started running barefoot around the grave.

"*Yakamashii* (too loud)!" muttered the annoyed captain, and one of the soldiers yelled at Grandma Dolbae and shoved her up the mountain.

After positioning her by a cliff, he aimed his rifle at her but stopped short. A cruel smile spread across his face. He let his rifle down and instead ruthlessly kicked her in the back.

Grandma Dolbae rolled down the mountain like a rock. Mountain birds flew up from where she had fallen. The women shivered at the sight. As if in a trance, they grasped the hoes and shovels that the soldiers handed them and started digging the grave that was covered with fresh dirt.

They removed the soil, brushed aside birch bark and pulled off the cloth that covered the corpses. Bodies that didn't even look like humans lay in the grave. Sobs that were unable to be stifled slipped out of some of the women. The women were told to drag the corpses out of the pit. As the Japanese soldiers barked at them, the women removed all the corpses from the grave and piled them up beside the pit.

One of the soldiers brought the green can again. He poured the gasoline over the corpses and lit them on fire. A pillar of smoke arose, and a sharp smell stung the women's noses. The smell of burning flesh tore apart the women's hearts.

Another hysterical wail arose from the group of women. As the smoke rose to the top of the pine trees, Kkeutsun opened her eyes wide and followed its trace. Tilting her head up to look at the black smoke draped over the blue sky like a mesh curtain, she felt a cold shiver run through her. She asked herself if she was still in her nightmare. But she could definitely hear someone crying and smell the burning flesh.

Is this horrible terror of a nightmare really happening to me?

The fear that penetrated her bones raised goosebumps on her flesh. As if to wake from this terrifying nightmare, Kkeutsun moaned and took a few steps back. Without realizing, she'd stepped down a bit from the crowd. The soldiers' eyes were still glued to the burning corpses, and they didn't notice Kkeutsun slipping away from the group. The moment she realized how far she was from the soldiers, Kkeutsun turned around and ran.

"*Sono onna o tsukamaeyo* (catch that bitch)!"

A shout rang out from behind her. Kkeutsun knew they were shouting at her, and she turned her head around for a moment. One of the soldiers was pointing at her, and two started running in her direction. Kkeutsun was scared out of her wits to see the men glowering at her like wild animals and charging toward her.

"Oh no!" she yelped and started running. She didn't know where she was going. The only thing she knew was that she needed to get out of that hellish place. Barely managing her heavy body, she clenched her teeth and ran as fast as she could.

Soon she was down the mountainside, heading toward

another hill in front of the village. It was where Deer Rock was—the rock that gave Deer Valley its name. The villagers thought of the rock as the guardian of their village. Some prayed to it, considering it a sacred rock that granted women's wishes to give birth to boys.

Kkeutsun felt as though she might be able to wake from this nightmare if she could get to Deer Rock. Perhaps the legendary deer would stand tall with its antlers and fight against the devils to protect her. Perhaps it would carry her tired and heavy body on its soft back and get her far, far away from there.

"*Tomare! Tomarankai utsuzo* (if you don't stop, we'll shoot)!"

She heard the frightful shouts between panting. It was so close, like a barking dog about to leap up on her back. But Kkeutsun kept on running.

Crack! A gunshot rang out, and Kkeutsun fell as if someone had hit her leg with a club. Instinctively, she wrapped her arms around her belly to protect the baby and fell on her side. Groaning, she struggled to get back on her feet with all her strength. Only after she took a few steps did she feel pain in her leg. The bottom half of her calf was covered in blood. Dragging her injured leg, she kept on running.

She ran, trying her best not to black out even though she could feel her consciousness slipping away. Her rubber shoe felt slippery from the blood that ran down her leg into it.

A narrow path lay in the grass-covered mountain edge like a part in a head of hair, and an oxcart was slowly rattling along on it. This path was the only way out of the village in this deep, remote valley.

Kkeutsun struggled to run toward the oxcart. Someone jumped off the oxcart with a look of surprise.

"Goodness me, aren't you Kkeutsun?"

It was Pastor Jang. He traveled the distance every week from Longjing to Deer Valley for worship services in the village. He not only gave great sermons but also explained the rage felt by Japan's enemies at the theft of Korea's national sovereignty and the necessity of Korean independence in a way that was easy for all to understand. Everyone in the village respected this good man. He was a close friend of Principal Ryang and had even filled in a few times as a substitute teacher when some of the teachers had to miss school.

"Pastor! Oh, Pastor Jang!"

Kkeutsun grasped his wrist, as if she were reunited with someone who'd saved her life. Her legs gave in, and she fell to the ground. Pastor Jang helped her up, and the oxcart driver helped her onto the cart.

The Japanese soldiers' shouts rang out through the air.

Upon seeing bloody Kkeutsun and the Japanese soldiers running toward them with swords and rifles, Pastor Jang realized the gravity of the situation.

"Please take care of Kkeutsun," Pastor Jang spoke to the oxcart driver. "Ride as fast as you can."

The driver hurriedly turned the ox around, pulling on the reins and lashing at its back with the willow branch in his hand.

"Come on, come on! Run quick!"

The driver's voice sounded strangely distorted with fear.

The ox began to run through the mountain at the driver's lashing. The rattling of the cart woke Kkeutsun up from a short blackout. She managed to sit up and turn around.

Pastor Jang was running toward the soldiers.

"What's going on? Why are you chasing after a

pregnant woman?"

"Doke (out of the way)!"

The soldiers bellowed savagely at the pastor, but he stood blocking them like a wall. One of the soldiers got down on one knee and fired his rifle at the retreating oxcart.

Crack!

Kkeutsun heard the bullet whiz above her head. She shivered at the loud gunshot that kept on ringing in her ears.

"What the hell!"

The oxcart driver threw away the willow branch in his hand and jumped off the oxcart.

The soldier loaded his rifle again and aimed it at Kkeutsun who sat still on the oxcart, staring blankly. At that moment, Pastor Jang threw himself on the soldier and grabbed the barrel of his firearm, pushing it up toward the sky.

Crack! A bullet tore through the air.

"Chikusho (curse you)! *Shinitainoka* (you want to die)?"

The soldier booted Pastor Jang in the stomach. Pastor Jang grabbed the soldier's foot and hung on. He held fast with all the strength he could muster. He didn't let go even as he was being dragged along the ground. Enraged, the soldier held up the rifle upside down and stabbed Pastor Jang in the shoulder with the bayonet. Yet even then, Pastor Jang's hands were clutched firmly around the soldier's ankle. Other soldiers surrounded him and began to stab him with their bayonets.

Kkeutsun heard Pastor Jang scream from behind. He was waving his hands in the air as black blood glugged out of his mouth and spurted from the stab wounds.

As the life poured out of his body, Pastor Jang bellowed one last time, "You sons of a venomous snake!"

Kkeutsun watched all of this unfold from the oxcart with her eyes widened in surprise. The ox was slowly pulling the cart along, unaware of the disaster taking place around it.

Pastor Jang stopped moving. A soldier kicked him over the ridge, and his body tumbled down. *Ptui!* The soldier spat on the man's bloodied body.

The soldiers were about to aim at the oxcart again but stopped. The cart was loudly rattling along, but there was no one on it. The soldiers rushed over and pulled on the reins. The ox stopped short. To the left there was a steep mountain slope that descended to a river with a strong

current, splashing waves and foam. The soldiers slung
their rifles over their shoulders and leaned over to look
down the slope, but no matter how hard they looked, they
couldn't see Kkeutsun.

"*Chikusho*! Where did she go? Hope she fell in the river
and died!"

The soldiers jabbered on for a bit and fired down the
mountain slope a few times. Bullets tore through azaleas,
scattering the flower petals in the air. Startled mountain
birds flew up into the sky, filling the mountainside with
chirps.

The soldiers searched the mountainside for a while
but turned around without finding Kkeutsun, who
was hiding inside a copse of bushes at the foot of the
mountain. Blood trickled down from the bullet wound in
her calf and soaked the ground, but she didn't dare treat
the wound. She could still hear the occasional murmurs
in Japanese from the top of the hill.

Engulfed in extreme terror, Kkeutsun was trembling as
if she'd come down with a chill. She only stared blankly
at the blood oozing from her leg. She felt both nauseated
and thirsty.

The sun's rays were much stronger, pouring a pool of

light over her head as she hid in the shade. Afraid that the Japanese soldiers might spot her, she kept on crouching further and further inside the bushes.

When the silence had continued for a while, Kkeutsun stretched out her neck and peeked out of the vegetation she was hiding in. On their way back to the village, the soldiers had stopped by Pastor Jang. Noticing that he was still alive, one of the soldiers pointed his rifle at the pastor's head.

Crack!

A flock of buntings flapped their wings and flew into the air.

Hoot! Hoot!

A scops owl continued to cry as though it were mourning for the widows who no longer had the energy to shed even a single a tear.

With a trembling hand, Kkeutsun took one corner of the train of her tattered skirt up to her lips. She clasped it between her chattering teeth and snapped her head to one side, ripping the cloth and revealing her underwear and pale thighs. But this was no time to fret about such things.

She tied the strip of cloth over the gunshot wound on

her leg. Then she let out a pained moan. It wasn't the pain in her leg. She felt something much more intense in her belly. It was so bad that Kkeutsun fell over backwards. The pain crawled up from her belly and enveloped her entire body. She dropped her jaw at the extreme pain, wide enough to show the roof of her mouth.

The mountain peak on which Deer Rock rested reflected in her eyes, as if it were going to fall down on her. She then noticed the black smoke that was rising from the valley and covering the sky. Sorrow and pain welled in her heart and rose up to her throat like a warm clot of blood. She couldn't even take a breath because of the pain that shot up from her belly.

"Oh, mother!"

Kkeutsun let out a scream in pain, calling for the mother she didn't even remember, who had died when she was an infant in swaddling clothes.

Barely holding onto consciousness, she caught sight of the azaleas in full bloom that covered the mountain slope. She flailed her arm and managed to grasp a branch of an azalea bush. She squeezed the branch with all her strength, uprooting the whole plant. She felt a hot ball of fire rising from around her bellybutton. Steamy heat burned near her stomach, and she writhed on the ground, digging her fingers into the dirt in pain.

With a gut-wrenching scream, Kkeutsun pushed out an ill-fortuned baby from the day of her birth, covered in scarlet blood as vivid as the azaleas all around her. As her taut belly began to relax, she took the baby between the train of her skirt with metallic tasting blood on her lips from biting down hard in pain. She held the wriggling infant in her arms and severed the umbilical cord with her teeth. Even amidst all this, her eyes scanned the baby's lower body. It was a girl.

Kkeutsun felt hot tears rolling down her face. She thought that she'd wept herself dry, but the tears flooded her eyes yet again as if they would not stop. She touched the baby's face with her tear-stained cheek. The baby flinched and let out its first cry.

Startled at the baby's loud cry bursting forth from its budlike lips, Kkeutsun quickly held her against her chest in a tight embrace. She was flustered as she looked around for any sign of noise or movement. Thankfully the Japanese soldiers were long gone.

The riverside was as quiet as death. Only azaleas were in full bloom all around, in the mountains in front of her, in the hill to her back, and in the sunlight and in the shades. Azaleas covered the ridges and peaks of the mountains, raised their heads from between rocks, and even spilled all the way down around the village.

But the village whose edges used to be resplendently embroidered with azaleas was no more. The river breeze that brushed Kkeutsun's cheeks was mixed with a scent of azaleas. She dried her tears in the touch of the consoling breeze.

Hoot! Hoot! From a distance, a disconsolate scops owl continued to cry in sorrow.

Flower Grave

Azaleas were in full bloom all around. Chunja stood on top of a straw bag with a dirt-covered knife in her hand. She had been digging for wild vegetables and only stood up to give her aching back a rest. But she stopped short, dazzled by the azaleas ablaze all around the foot of the mountain.

Completely speechless, sixteen-year-old Chunja, clad in white cotton summer *jeogori* and a black cotton skirt that fell to her ankles, stared agape at the resplendent feast of flowers.

Azaleas blossomed on their own, like an abandoned wife giving birth all alone, in the empty valley where no one ever looked. But when they were in full bloom all around the edge of the mountains, like spilled paint, they captivated anyone who laid eyes on them. The hillside was covered with azaleas, and their bushes were in bloom at the entrance of the mountain path, on the embankment between fields, and in other spots where the sunlight shone all day long.

Flaring her nostrils to take in the scent of the flowers and narrowing her eyes against the bright sunlight that tickled her eyelids, Chunja looked down from the mountain. Beneath her feet, a beautiful landscape lay like an unfurled painting.

Rice paddies stretched out across the land, beyond where the eyes could see. They'd been irrigated with the water from the river and cultivated by people clad in white, who'd moved to the valley that had only known farming on unirrigated fields. A narrow river cut across the fields, glistening in the sunlight like a silver sword. The willows lining the riverside were budding with fresh green leaves, and the warm breeze was making the soil swell back into life like steamed rice cakes.

A carpet of rice plants already transplanted into paddies were green with vigor. People said that this year's rice seedlings seemed healthier than the previous year's because the early spring thaw had allowed the rice seeds to be sowed early. Yellow oxen were grazing along the footpath around the rice paddies that were thickly lined with foxtails.

Chunja lightly pounded her legs with her fists to relieve the cramps caused by squatting for too long. Her eyes scanned the landscape and fell on the entrance of the pathway below the mountains. A mound caught her eyes. It was a flower grave. When her eyes landed on the grave, without thinking, Chunja let out a sigh as white as the bellflower root.

People said it had been there since around the time of Chunja's birth. The burial mound was tremendously large compared to regular graves. So big that people who didn't know better might mistake it for a hill. Located by the entrance of the village, the mound wasn't encircled by stones to mark it as a grave and there were no inscribed tombstones. But it was well tended. And it seemed to be growing bigger as people piled more dirt on it over time.

Since the grave was at the entrance of the village, people passed by it several times a day as they went out into the rice paddies or into town. Yet those who passed the grave didn't simply walk by it. It was impossible to walk past with indifference.

To Chunja, mound evoked fear and sorrow, which

had turned to hatred. She grew up watching the villagers down on their hands and knees in front of the grave and wailing until they ran out of breath around this time every year. When azaleas opened up their rueful and delicate petals, the grave became covered in the flowers that people would pick and offer to the dead.

And as azaleas bloomed and burgeoned, wails and cries that sounded like the pained howls of beasts that have lost their cubs or mates were heard all day long at the burial mound. All the women of the village hugged the grave and lamented as if to win a crying contest. Some even fainted from crying too hard.

Chunja's mom was also among the crying women. When the azaleas began to bloom, she cried all day. She would limp all the way to the grave and wring her tears out of her, crying a pitch above others with her already high-pitched voice. She cried, nearly fainting every time, grasping at the bristly dried grass covering the burial mound.

Chunja rarely saw her mom cry during the rest of the year. She was a tough woman who put food on the table despite her disability, so she didn't even have the time to cry. Crying was a luxury she couldn't afford.

But one day a year, her mom plopped down in front of the burial mound as if she'd given up everything in life and shed all the tears she would cry for the entire year.

Her wails were so heartbreaking that young Chunja couldn't even bring herself to console her mom. Without knowing what prompted the tears, she only stood by the burial mound to cry with the rest of the adults.

Even the cuckoo birds joined in. Like the cry of the cuckoo, which sounded as though it were coughing up blood full of resentment and tears, the women let out desperate and piercing wails, but Chunja didn't know the whole truth behind the mourning.

There was another grave, not far from the huge burial mound. It was much smaller than the massive one by the village entrance, but there was a chiseled stone table in front of it as well as a tombstone. The tombstone was engraved with the words "Grave of Reverend Jang Indeok."

When she was done with her blood-curdling wails, Kkeutsun would grab Chunja's hand and visit the small grave. She'd push down the reluctant Chunja's head and kick at her calves to make her kneel in front of the grave and bow.

Chunja used to ask, "Mom, whose grave is this?"

But her mother never gave an answer. Instead, she would take off the towel she'd been wearing on her head and wipe the tombstone clean as if it were their living room floor. Kkeutsun would wipe the dust off each line that was etched into the tombstone. Every few years, looking at the words that had begun to fade, she said, "I should put some black ink here. It's been years, and now the colors are fading and you can't even see all the words."

After she was done cleaning the tombstone, she'd once again be filled with emotion and cry into the towel.

Chunja was eventually able to read the words on the tombstone when she learned to read and write at the night school. But even now, she didn't know whose grave this was or why her mom made her come bow in front of it after the ritual in front of the massive burial mound. Yet she didn't want to ask who it was either. The huge burial mound at the village entrance and the small one were both simply horrid and terrifying to young Chunja.

Chunja noticed a bouquet of azaleas in front of the tombstone at the small grave. There was someone with his head bowed in front of the grave. She heard quiet sobs when the direction of the wind changed.

The person who had been praying silently straightened his back and held up his head. There were tears in the corners of his pearly black eyes. At that moment Chunja's heart began to pound. It was her teacher. He was the young unmarried teacher at the night school and a deacon at the local church.

On one spring evening, Chunja's old aunt, who had been living at Chunja's, smiled and said, "Chunja, now you won't have to listen to Grandma Hoeryeong make up stories anymore. They say there's going to be a night school in the village."

"Really?" asked Chunja, a spark of excitement rising from her heart. "Is that true?"

Chunja had never even been near a school because her family was too poor. And there were no schools in Deer Valley. People said there used to be a fancy school, but the Japanese people set fire to it and burned it down before Chunja was born. It was impossible for children to walk the several miles from the remote village of Deer Valley, deep in the mountains, to a school in the nearby town. So aside from a few children from families that were relatively well off, most stayed illiterate well into their young adulthood, like Chunja.

"The church is going to set up a school for free. They've even invited a teacher from Longjing."

"Really?" asked Chunja again, kicking off the quilted comforter she'd covered her cold feet with. It was certainly welcome news to Chunja, who had to quench her thirst for knowledge with stories about ghosts in wells and other old folktales told by Grandma Hoeryeong, known as a storyteller in the village, although not a great one.

"He went to Eunjin Middle School in Longjing. Apparently, he even speaks Russian, Japanese, and Chinese."

Happiness spread across old auntie's face, as she said that now children would be able to learn to read at least.

"What would girls do with studying?" Chunja's mother snorted, massaging her bad leg that ached on rainy days.

"But you wouldn't want to leave your only daughter completely illiterate, would you?"

At the aunt's words, Chunja's mom brusquely responded as though she were sick of hearing about it. "Don't use big words with me, sister. How fortunate that she was born without losing an eye or an ear during that madness! What good would studying do a girl, anyway?

Even if she goes to school, she'll be nothing more than a sow that can read."

"Well…" Chunja's chatterbox of an aunt grew quiet at Kkeutsun's snappish reply.

Nevertheless, Chunja was full of anticipation.

A few days later, she met the new teacher. Not only girls and boys Chunja's age, but also all the adults of the village gathered at the church at the teacher's request. The church had been rebuilt with the help of Canadian missionaries several years after the Japanese soldiers had massacred the village.

The night school teacher from Longjing stood at the lectern.

"Hello everyone. It's nice to meet you. My name is Jang Mo-se."

The teacher was a young man in his mid-twenties, neatly clad in a brown suit the color of a chestnut. He bowed to the villagers.

"He's young."

"Goodness, he's handsome."

The villagers murmured as they continued to stare with curiosity at the smartly dressed night school teacher.

Chunja's eyes were set on the buttons on the night

school teacher's shirt, which was buttoned all the way up to his neck. The fastenings sparkled even in the dim light of the oil lamp, and Chunja thought that they resembled stars in the night sky.

"Teacher, you have a strange name. Mo-se? What does it mean?"

Curious villagers asked about the teacher's unusual name.

"Are you named after Mo-se (Korean for Moses) in the Bible? The man who parted the sea?" asked the wife of Deacon Heo.

"My father gave me the name," the night school teacher responded with a smile. "Mo means 'end' and se means 'year.' He named me Mo-se because I was born at the end of the year."

After giving this answer, he spoke as if to himself, "But perhaps he named me after Moses in the Bible, hoping that I'd grow up to be someone who was likewise exceptional."

"What a great father."

In no time, the villagers were bedazzled by the gentle-spoken and neatly dressed young night school teacher.

"So what's a night school?" asked one of the villagers.

A smile spread across the teacher's lips as he looked at people's simple and honest faces.

"Why don't I sing you a song first?" asked the teacher in lieu of a reply.

"Sounds great!"

"Sure! Let's see how great a singer the new teacher is!"

People seemed overjoyed at the young teacher's willingness to sing for them without being prompted. Numerous sets of eyes full of curiosity and expectations landed on him.

After first clearing his throat, the teacher began to sing.

From every stormy wind that blows,
From every swelling tide of woes,
There is a calm, a sure retreat—
'Tis found beneath the mercy seat.

It was a Christian hymn called "From Every Stormy Wind That Blows." People who knew the song began to sing with him. Chunja also sang along.

A round of applause followed the song.

"Encore! Encore!"

"Let's learn new songs later and sing them together,"

said the teacher as he pushed back a lock of hair that fell over his forehead with his forefinger. A smile as warm as the sun's rays lit up his face the whole time.

"Encore! Encore!"

Charmed by the teacher's beautiful voice, the villagers requested another song.

At their insistence, the teacher said, "All right. I'll sing another one."

Vroom, vroom, roaring cars drive on,
Roads that the laborers have paved.
Yet a man who had idled drives on by
Leaving the laborers angry and betrayed.

At the more solemn expression and lyrics delivered by a lower tone of voice, the church that had been brimming with excitement became silent within moments.

Hungry, we grow rice with blood and sweat
But not a bowl of rice comes our way
A man who knows nothing of paddies and rice
Eats and fattens as he lazes around all day.

On the third floor of a tall building
A dog full of mutton snoozes snug and warm
While a man begging for a spoonful of rice
lies starving at the gate in a snowstorm.

A man's storehouse reeks of rotting rice
While starving people work without breaks
His neighbor's child cries for rice,
And the listening passerby's heart aches.

The teacher sang the song in a quiet voice. He sang all four verses by heart. His voice was low, but his song resonated like waves in people's hearts. Some of the women wiped the tears from corners of their eyes with the long sashes of their *jeogori*. Forgetting even to clap, they stared at the teacher with faces deep in thought.

"Ladies and gentlemen!"

The teacher who was done singing scanned the room.

"Starting tomorrow, this church will also be used as a classroom for the night school. Before we begin classes tomorrow, I'd like to give everyone homework. So please listen and think about what I tell you."

Calmly gazing at the villagers, he continued, "You see,

even if we cultivate the land all year long, working until the scorching sun burns a hole on our heads, we can't even eat a spoonful of white rice. Even if we go around working all day for an entire year carrying A-frames on our backs, we can't even save a single coin. Why do you think it's this way?"

The teacher looked around the room as if asking someone to give him an answer. But no one stepped up with a clear answer. The teacher answered his own question.

"This is all because of the Walbon people. The Walbon people have stolen our home from us. They're our enemies who bleed us dry, strip the skin off our backs, and gnaw on our bones. We're all people who have crossed the river to get here. And anyone who crossed a river knows that they die if they stay still under water. You can only find a way to live when you struggle."

"Um, teacher."

Someone interrupted the young teacher. It was Chunja's chatterbox auntie. Chunja was embarrassed by her aunt's interrupting the teacher's lofty speech.

"You keep saying Walbon, Walbon. What does Walbon mean?"

A smile spread across the teacher's lips once again.

"You know the Chinese character for Ilbon (Japan)? The first character is *il* (日). Well, try stomping on it really hard."

The teacher picked up his leg and pretended to crush something on the ground with an exaggerated motion.

"When you do that, the character for *il* gets squashed into *wal* (日). It's completely flattened."

Laughter erupted from the crowd.

"Walbon! That's funny."

"Those Walbon bastards are really squashed, aren't they?"

Once the people settled down, the teacher continued.

"Haven't we lost our fathers, husbands, and brothers to those Walbon bastards? We can't take back our homeland, the land of milk and honey, with our tears and laments alone. We have to unite and fight to get out from under the rule of the Walbon people and gain our freedom. To do this, we have to learn first. It's hard and some of you may think that it's unnecessary, but without learning, we cannot talk of liberation. We cannot talk of happiness. And so we should not be lazy to learn. Have you looked at the mountains and fields of your village recently? Have you seen the azaleas bloom all over the mountain? Even in the deep mountain valleys, even in the toughest conditions, azaleas bloom, shining brightly with passion all across the mountains! Let us be like the blossoming azaleas in accomplishing our tasks."

The teacher spoke in earnest with his hands balled up into fists. His voice had grown louder with passion, and his eyes sparkled ever brighter with vigor.

With her eyes widened like a chipmunk's, Chunja stared at the teacher as though she'd fallen under a spell. In the room where the kerosene lamp created waves of light, only the teacher seemed to shine brightly. He was handsome enough to make her legs wobble by just looking at him, and Chunja could even see something like a halo forming around him.

After returning home, Chunja lit a kerosene lamp by the wood-burning stove and sat down. She'd come home, hugging the book that the teacher had given out to the students. It was a textbook that had been neatly handwritten in ink and copied. To prevent the students from mistakenly switching textbooks, the teacher had written each student's name on the cover.

"What's your name?"

When the teacher—the young, handsome bachelor teacher—approached Chunja and asked her name, Chunja became so flustered that she couldn't answer right away. She started as if she had been burned upon hearing his voice from so close. She was sure that not only her face but her whole body was flushed out of embarrassment.

"What happened, did you go and swallow your name whole, like a chipmunk with a nut?" said Chunja's aunt as she poked Chunja's side and answered for her. "It's Chunja. Lee Chunja."

"Chunja? Chun means spring. It's a great name."

The teacher uncapped his fountain pen with his mouth and neatly wrote Chunja's name in a corner of the textbook. The sound of the pen scratching paper made her heart flutter.

Chunja looked at her name on the cover of the textbook, poring over each stroke. It was the first time she'd seen the three characters of her name written down. She kept stroking her textbook.

Chun means spring. It's a great name. She could still hear the teacher's voice, gently swaying like grass in a breeze. The words that reached every corner of her heart and the sound of the pen nib scratching the paper continued to echo in her mind.

Her mother, who had gone to bed early instead of attending the assembly at the night school, stirred and asked, "Did you pick up a treasure chest or something? What are you staring at?"

"It's a book the new night school teacher gave us," answered Chunja, unable to tear her eyes still from the textbook.

"Go to sleep already," Kkeutsun said testily. "Kerosene isn't cheap."

But Chunja couldn't fall asleep because the images of the night school and the bachelor teacher remained so vivid in her mind. The shiny, broad forehead, thick eyebrows, high nose, and the perfect line of his lips underneath. He was a handsome bachelor. His face lingered in her mind.

What a strange name he had. I'd never heard anything like it before.

Chunja quietly mouthed his name, "Jang... Mo... Se..."

Her cheeks immediately blushed scarlet, and she covered them with her hands.

You know the Chinese character for Ilbon (Japan)? The

first character is il (日). *Well, try stomping on it really hard. When you do that, the character for* il *gets squashed into* wal (曰). *It's completely flattened.*

Remembering his funny explanation of the word Walbon, Chunja let out a laugh.

"What's wrong with you? Laughing out of the blue in the middle of the night?"

Kkeutsun sat up and blew out the lamp.

A few days later, Chunja made small pancakes. They were flower pancakes. She'd roamed around the mountains, breaking off branches of azaleas. She carefully chose the ones with full centers and well-formed petals. She then picked the flowers off the branches. After that, she pulled on the flower cups, which came apart from the flowers with the stamens. Chunja took the stamen-less flowers and rinsed them in cold water. After draining them in a colander, she placed them in a sunny corner of the yard to dry. While the flowers were drying, she brought out a scoop of glutinous rice flour from the storehouse and poured boiling water on it. Then she kneaded the mixture until the dough became smooth and elastic. Afterward, she placed a damp cotton cloth over the bowl containing the dough.

A while later, she tore off balls of dough the size of quail eggs and molded them into a round and flat shape. She then placed the flattened balls of dough on the heated griddle. For each one, when the under-side was cooked, she flipped it over, placed an azalea flower on it, and waited for the other side to cook through.

"If we had some honey, I could've dabbed a bit on each one…"

She gave one to her mom for a taste.

"It probably won't taste like anything because I cooked it without even a little bit of sesame oil," Chunja said out of embarrassment, as she finished cooking the rest.

Chunja was sorry for using the rice flour that her mom saved for special occasions. She was also sorry that she cooked them without even a drop of sesame oil, and that she didn't have honey to dip the pancakes in.

But her mom didn't say anything, as if she knew why Chunja was making the flower pancakes. On any other day, Kkeutsun would've roared at Chunja, making dust fall from the ceiling, "Have you been possessed by the ghost of someone who starved to death? How are you always lusting after food?"

The azalea pancakes tasted a bit sour. But Chunja

thought she could taste a bit of sweetness from all the hard work she'd put into it. Above all, the golden-brown pancakes topped with flowers were too beautiful to eat.

"My word, the young teacher is Pastor Jang's son," said Kkeutsun to Chunja, as she sat cooking the flower pancakes. "Remember Pastor Jang? He's the one who saved my life!"

One day, Kkeutsun had told Chunja about the big and small burial mounds at the entrance of the village. Showing her the terrible gunshot wound that almost looked as if a huge beast had taken a bite of her calf, Kkeutsun told Chunja about Pastor Jang.

"When you see the teacher, make sure to say hello. He's young as a spring chicken, but he's as wise as an owl. He went to a good school and is even a deacon of the church. On top of that, he's the son of our savior. If it weren't for Pastor Jang, you would not be here. You wouldn't even have been born."

As Chunja placed the pancakes in a wooden bowl and wrapped it in cloth, she listened to her mother's words that touched her heart like a warm breeze.

In the evening, Chunja headed to the church, treading on the moonlit path, with the pancakes wrapped in cloth.

The young teacher's residence was on the edge of the church grounds. The wooden bowl wasn't heavy at all, but her footsteps were hesitant. She kept on thinking, "I should've put them in a prettier bowl." The thought of the pancakes in a rough wooden receptacle kept weighing on her mind.

She didn't have any pretty bowls at home. She and her mom often ate straight out of the pot, sitting around the stove, or out of a gourd used for scooping water. Chunja was downcast about her wretched life, where she couldn't even have pretty bowls full of delicious food she could pick at, as though playing house.

The teacher lived at the foot of the mountain behind the village where the cuckoo bird sang. Azaleas underneath the sorghum straw fence around his house seemed to brighten up the whole place. They were the azaleas that Chunja had placed there. Even until a few days ago, the branches were plain sticks with barely any buds, but the flowers were now shyly in full bloom, revealing their delicate colors like a bride about to step into a wedding hall.

Unlike flurried Chunja, the azaleas seemed to be at peace, without any hint of fear or anxiety, even at dusk.

Azaleas bear more flowers when the branches are snapped off. Squeezed between the slim stalks of sorghum in the fence, azaleas began to blossom a few flower buds at a time, casting off the cold, severe winter and lighting up the gloomy little town.

The village was quiet before the azaleas bloomed. But it wasn't desolate. It was the kind of quiet that presaged something unusual coming this way.

Chunja's heart, on the other hand, was far from quiet. It wasn't because the bowl was heavy. The closer she got to the teacher's house, the quicker her breath seemed to grow, and her heart pounded uncontrollably as though she'd hidden a rabbit in her bosom.

At the gate made out of twigs, Chunja stood on her tiptoes a while, peeking into the house that was lit up with a hemp stalk lamp, and finally worked up her courage to call the teacher.

"Teacher…"

Nothing stirred inside. Perhaps her voice was too small. She called him again.

"Teacher."

A familiar shadow emerged from behind the bedroom door, and the door opened. Soon the twig gate opened as well, and the teacher stepped out into the open.

"It's Chunja from the night school. It's just a little meager snack, but I hope you enjoy it."

Chunja had repeated the two sentences over and over on her way to his house, but the words seemed to get stuck in her throat.

With a quiet face marked by eyes that shone with goodness, the young teacher looked at her. Chunja immediately dropped her head and focused on the azaleas by the sorghum straw fence. Chunja stood for a moment, tucking the loose piece of hair that kept on slipping from behind her ears, and suddenly thrust the bowl into his chest, as if forcing him to take it. She turned around and started running.

"Thank you so much!"

Behind her, she could hear the teacher chuckling now and then.

"Why are you empty-handed? What did you do with the bowl? You forgot to bring it back, didn't you? Have you seen a more scatterbrained girl!"

Despite her mother's scolding, a subtle smile lingered in the corner of Chunja's lips.

When Chunja lifted her head and came out of her reverie, timidly wearing her affection in the corner of her lips, the teacher's shadow was gone from the grave. Picking up the basket of wild vegetables, Chunja walked through the forest and waded through the grass fields, finally reaching the foot of the mountain.

Noticing Chunja step through the door with a basket full of wild vegetables, Kkeutsun said, "He's gone. Pastor Jang's son."

"What?"

The dirt-covered knife fell from Chunja's hand.

Chunja rushed outside. With her hands grasping the twig gate, she looked out toward the entrance of the village, as far as her eyes could reach.

By the corner of the mountain that the young teacher passed by, a cluster of azaleas were abloom in dazzling white.

A Hymn on a Moonlit Night

To the poor, azaleas were flowers to be feared. They heralded the dreadful time of the year when all the stored grains had been used up and there was nothing left to eat.

Only a few people consciously associated azaleas with hunger, but nevertheless it was true. They were flowers that signaled the period of spring poverty, known as the "barley hump"—a time when all the stored grains have been consumed and the barley is not ready for harvest yet). And around this time, there was something that filled Chunja with fear. It was her mother nagging at her and sending her to her aunt's place in Hoemakdong (Tumen).

Most kids liked going to see their mother's family, but Chunja was an exception. She didn't just dislike going there; she was as afraid to go as if it were the home of

Yeomna, a king of the underworld.

Chunja's gruff mother wasn't sending her daughter to her sister's place to indulge in luxury. There was a reason Kkeutsun repeatedly badgered her daughter to go to her sister's house—it was to beg for money.

Chunja's aunt ran a lodging house in Hoemakdong, by the corner of the road that led to the county of Onseong, over the border in Korea, and was financially far better off than Chunja and her mother, who worked the rice paddies for a living.

Kkeutsun's family barely made ends meet. There were only women in the household, and they lived hand to mouth even though they worked their fingers to the bone every day from dawn until dusk. It was possible to endure the hard work, but the period of the barley hump was a difficult hurdle to overcome. There was therefore no other way than to put on a brazen face and stretch out their empty hands.

At first, Kkeutsun herself went a few times to borrow money, but once Chunja blossomed into a young woman she made her go.

The first time she left for her aunt's house, Chunja had been excited to leave Deer Valley for the first time ever.

But after that first time, Chunja had refused to go again. Sure enough, her aunt's family had humiliated her for coming to beg for money.

Chunja would never forget the mean looks they'd given her. When she'd arrived at her aunt's house, her uncle was eating, but he didn't even ask Chunja whether she'd had a meal or suggest that she come eat with him. Her aunt's gestures as she washed the dishes were gruff as well. The bowls clattered against each other as though she were going to break them.

When Chunja refused to go to her aunt's house, Kkeutsun swore at her, but even then Chunja kept on refusing and ended up getting a thrashing. Kkeutsun was as thin as a shrike, but she armed herself with invisible thorns, perhaps because of her limp, and so she was second to none in the village when it came to her temper.

"Then we'll both just starve to death. We're on the verge of dying of hunger and you have the luxury of saying no? Where did you get your brains from, stupid?"

Kkeutsun grasped and pulled at Chunja's hair, but Chunja clenched her teeth and staunchly refused. She was normally the kind of girl who would set out to pick wild raspberries even in winter if her mom asked her to.

But she'd steadfastly refused to go to her aunt's place, and as a result they just managed to survive last year's barley hump by a hair's breadth.

As that dangerous time came around again this year, Kkeutsun geared up and asked Chunja.

"Are you going to go to Hoemakdong? Yes or no?"

But at Chunja's response, Kkeutsun stared at her with her mouth agape, unable to say what she'd prepared to say.

"Yes mom, I'll go," Chunja said meekly.

The next day, Chunja started on her way to Hoemakdong. She'd washed her bobbed hair at the well and combed it; her skirt may have been frayed and worn, but she'd at least washed it clean.

Seeing Chunja set off hastily from home, Kkeutsun looked as if she'd seen a ghost.

A new bridge was being built across the Tumen River that flowed between Hoemakdong in China and Onseong in Korea, and some of the laborers at the construction site were from Deer Valley. Chunja boarded the oxcart along with those laborers and started on her long journey.

Chunja had her own reason for making the journey to Hoemakdong, getting rocked and rattled on the oxcart all day long among middle-aged men reeking of the sour stench of sweat and breathing in dust rising from the dirt road. It was because the young teacher Jang Mo-se had gone to Hoemakdong to serve at a church there.

For a while, Mo-se's handsome figure kept lingering in her mind such that Chunja had been anxious to see him. But no one knew of her yearning for him. Her feelings for the young teacher were secret and spread unexpectedly, like the scarlet spot on a young girl's skirt when she has her first period and she doesn't want anyone finding out.

Leaving the village on the oxcart, Chunja felt a strange force grabbing her from behind. She turned around instinctively and saw that azaleas were in full bloom at the foot of the mountain that encircled her village, blossoming fiercely as though squeezing out all their energy for the last time.

When Chunja arrived in Hoemakdong, sure enough, her uncle and aunt eyed her coldly for having come during the barley hump. Only her cousin Gwang-ok, who was the same age as Chunja, welcomed her.

Her aunt's family had originally lived in Deer Valley too but moved to Hoemakdong several years ago to start their inn. Before they'd moved, Chunja and Gwang-ok had been good friends. With a darker skin tone resembling that of men who work outside all day and a tomboyish personality, Gwang-ok showed her white teeth as she flashed a wide smile at the unexpected arrival of Chunja.

In the evening, the two of them headed to the church. It was only about a stone's throw away from the inn Gwang-ok's family owned—Chunja could actually see the cross made of thuja wood on top of the church roof. When Chunja looked down from the inn, the church's windows were lit up at dusk. The house of worship sat by the riverside, and as a two-story red brick building it was incomparably bigger than its counterpart in Deer Valley. Most of all, this church had electricity, so it was far brighter than the one at Deer Valley, which was only lit with kerosene lamps. Brightly lit up even against the pitch-black night, the interior of the church seemed like a world in a dream.

Yellow lamp light emanated through the almond-shaped stained-glass window, as did the sound of soft singing. The warm rolling notes of a hymn enveloped the church like an aura, gently traversing through the cold night.

They barely made it out of the house under the aunt's watchful gaze and were late to church.

Chunja's aunt said, "We don't believe in God, like some crazy people do," so only Gwang-ok went, just for fun.

Chunja and Gwang-ok took off their shoes, held them in their hands and tiptoed into the church. Inside, the red brick structure was crowded with people attending the service. But even among the crowd of people, Chunja's eyes immediately landed on Mo-se. Chunja couldn't take her eyes off him.

Mo-se had just finished his sermon and was stepping down from the lectern. He approached the harmonium, which was placed a step down from the simple pulpit. He stood there with one hand on the musical instrument.

The organist opened the harmonium lid. Then she and Mo-se made eye contact. The woman's hands descended slowly on the keys. Beautiful music bounced out of the harmonium like waterdrops. The young teacher's soft voice became entwined with the melody like silk.

...he makes me lie down in green pastures,
He leads me beside quiet waters
He restores my soul.

He guides me along the right paths
For the glory of the Lord.

Within moments Chunja became absorbed in the song. In sync with each note of the melody, she moved step by step into a dream.

In the dream, she saw herself being led by someone's hand through the green pastures. She could see a spring in front of her. The person who had been holding her hand scooped water from the spring in a glass bowl. Then he poured the liquid as clear and pure as holy water on top of Chunja's head. Enraptured, Chunja received the holy water with her whole body. It warmed her. The person who was pouring the sacred liquid on Chunja was none other than Mo-se.

Chunja awoke from her trance when she felt a jab in her side. It was Gwang-ok.

"Look at the woman playing the harmonium," she whispered to Chunja after poking her in the ribs a few times. "Isn't she pretty?"

At her words, Chunja tore her wholehearted gaze

away from Mo-se. The woman who was playing the harmonium while the teacher sang was certainly beautiful.

"She'd even make the legendary Chinese consort Yang Guifei cry out of envy, don't you think?" Gwang-ok half stood from her seat and whispered into Chunja's ear.

Above the black choir robe stuck the white collar of the woman's summer jacket, which propped up her lily-white face like a flower cup. Her beautiful pale visage was also embraced by a ring of lovely, voluminous black hair. Enraptured by the music, her eyes were quietly closed, and her eyelashes stretched out like the eaves of a house. The fingers pressing down on each key were slender and long, like lotus stems. Trim, elegant, beautiful, and holy… a member of the choir so beautiful that not even all the best adjectives in the world were enough to describe her looks as she played the harmonium.

The instrument was glowing gold from the light from the bare bulb. Underneath it, the organist's two little feet danced over the pedals. As her hands and feet moved in rhythm, beautiful sounds emerged.

"She's Park Yeongsin, an important member of the church's choir," Gwang-ok whispered again.

A gentleman sitting in front of them turned around and shushed them with a finger to his lips. Gwang-ok stuck out her tongue in embarrassment.

But unable to keep quiet for too long, Gwang-ok once again whispered into Chunja's ear.

"That woman, Park Yeongsin, she's the third daughter of the pastor of this church. That's why she shines like that."

Gwang-ok continued to whisper excitedly, but Chunja's gaze was solely focused on Mo-se.

"You know they say like attracts like. Yeongsin over there is apparently Deacon Jang's girlfriend."

Chunja, who had been letting her cousin's words go in one ear and go out the other with her eyes glued to Mo-se, snapped her head toward Gwang-ok at those words. She stared hard at the girl.

"What?" she nearly shouted without realizing.

The eyes of the people in the pew in front of them turned to them at once.

Chunja didn't know how long the sermon went on. She didn't know how many times the choir sang. When night fell, the members of the congregation left the church and returned home. Only Chunja remained in the churchyard.

She had told Gwang-ok that she'd like to pass some news from home to Deacon Jang, and Gwang-ok left alone. She didn't seem worried about heading home by herself this late since her house was so close. But before she disappeared out of sight, Gwang-ok turned around and asked, "Are you all right?"

She must have noticed that Chunja had become visibly downcast during the sermon. Chunja forced a smile. Then she shook her head like Cain, hiding his bloodied hands behind him and denying his part in killing his brother Abel, right after burying him in the ground.

Mo-se and the choir member Yeongsin were the only ones left in the church. They closed the harmonium lid and put a small lock on it. They tidied up the seat cushions and swept the floor with a small broom. They were the last ones to leave the building.

Mo-se locked the door to the church and handed over the key to Yeongsin. When they stepped outside, Chunja quickly hid herself behind a willow tree in the churchyard.

The couple didn't return home right away. Instead,

they sat shoulder to shoulder on the church steps.

Blood rushed to Chunja's face and her pulse quickened. She became breathless and felt her chest tighten.

It was a moonlit night, and a narrow-mouthed toad that must have awoken from its winter sleep before all the other toads gave its croaky call. The moon that had brightly illuminated the churchyard disappeared when Mo-se and Yeongsin emerged. It was as if the moon were hiding to hide their tryst from the eyes of the villagers. Snug darkness enveloped them and Chunja too, who was embarrassingly trapped behind the tree, unable to come or go.

"Do you have to go?" asked Yeongsin with her eyes on Mo-se. Her voice was subdued, different from her smooth singing voice that had belted out the hymn earlier.

Mo-se clutched Yeongsin's hands resting on her lap. Looking deep into her eyes, he said, "There is no end to the pursuit of spirituality. There is still a lot that I don't know, and I've become keenly aware of the need to study theology more. I want to come back to you, Yeongsin, as a proper minister. And when I do, your father will gladly welcome me."

Yeongsin let out an audible sigh, and Mo-se put his

arms around her shoulders.

"I'll only be away for a little while. It's not like I'm going away forever."

After another sigh, Yeongsin spoke.

"Soongsil School is run by foreign missionaries, and it's highly regarded, even in Pyongyang. When you graduate from there, you'll be a true Moses."

Yeongsin's cheeks glowed with a heartwarming smile. Her eyes sparkled with adoration.

"We're all looking for a true Moses to save our people from a pit of fire in these troubled times," said Mo-se, still holding Yeongsin's hands in his.

Yeongsin's face was troubled as she prepared to bid her lover farewell. She had been fidgeting with the buttons on her choir robe with her head bowed, when suddenly she spoke.

"Study hard, and when you come back, you must teach me the catechism."

"Teach, no, but let's certainly study it together," Mo-se readily answered. "These days, there are many problems that our sisters in faith face. Particularly in everyday life. I believe that people like us who are enlightened have to think about what must be done. This is something that my father grappled with for a long time and what I need to put into practice. My trip to the distant Deer Valley and my going to study at the school in Pyongyang are all part of that."

Yeongsin listened closely to his words.

"I believe in you," said Yeongsin as she once again looked up at Mo-se with tears in her eyes.

"Don't be so sad. Three years will pass quickly. And God will work through the Holy Spirit to provide us with the joy of reunion that is ten times, a hundred times bigger than the sorrow of our parting now."

Mo-se wiped the tears from the corners of Yeongsin's eyes with his hand.

Yeongsin said, "I'll think hard about what I need to do as I remain here. And I'll be praying for you."

She clasped her hands. Mo-se did the same with his.

"Our people are currently enveloped in the darkness," said Mo-se. "To overcome this darkness, we must absolutely believe in God's promise and love. Particularly when the darkness grows deeper and the night becomes longer. So let us pray. In times of trouble, let us just pray with all our hearts."

With their hands clasped together respectfully by their

chests, the two prayed quietly in the dark.

"Dear Lord, we can't see anything here right now. All we can see is the darkness full of suffering. Even though this place is full of contempt and disdain now, we want to believe that it will soon be transformed into the land of Your grace. Lord, please help us keep the faith. Amen!"

"Lord, please help us keep the faith. Amen!"

Upon finishing their prayer, Mo-se and Yeongsin rose from the steps and disappeared into the darkness.

After the couple vanished from sight like a mirage, the churchyard was as quiet as deep waters.

Even long after they left, Chunja didn't move a muscle as she stood behind the willow tree, seeming like a branch herself. Feeling like a corner of her heart had been ripped out, she placed her hand on her chest and pressed down.

She only came to her senses when the breeze from the river blew behind her, lifting the collar of her cotton *jeogori*. She felt that the weather—stuck between the spring and the summer—was colder than ever.

Chunja stood restlessly for a long time behind the tree and finally stepped out from behind it. She looked around, checking that no one else had been watching her act like an idiot.

Her empty stomach growled. She'd barely eaten the rice balls she'd brought on her journey, sitting squeezed between men all day long on the oxcart. She couldn't eat much even after she arrived in Hoemakdong, as she was on pins and needles because of her churlish uncle. But the emptiness of her heart that roared like the growling of her unfed belly outweighed her hunger.

Mo-se with another woman. Chunja couldn't help but think, *Was this it? Have I come riding on an oxcart the whole day long and all this way for this? Was this the reason why I picked flowers, made flower pancakes, cried when I said goodbye, and asked after the man who doesn't even know that I'm secretly in love with him?*

In the corner of her heart, she could still feel the excitement and passion she had felt when she'd left home, but the reality was quite different.

A narrow-mouthed toad croaked from somewhere.

Who could be so foolish like a toad? You're the foolish toad! Chunja could hear her mother's voice, scoffing at her as she often did.

Chunja thought, *She's right. I'm the foolish toad. You don't need to do something extremely idiotic to be a foolish toad. I'm certainly a foolish toad.*

Chunja let out a rueful laugh at herself.

Having fantasized about something that was clearly impossible, she felt like a foolish toad who cried after waking up too early from its winter sleep. It was like trying to measure the height of the sky with a stick. Recalling the dizzyingly beautiful face of Yeongsin, Chunja's shoulders sank out of a deep feeling of inferiority. Compared to the daughter of a minister with exceptional looks, Chunja was nothing. She was just a lousy and homely girl, a dunce, a foolish toad born to a country widow with a limp.

And the object of her affections was a handsome man who dreamed of becoming a minister, who was going to study at a college. He was also the son of the man who had saved her mother.

How could I possibly measure up to someone like that? Chunja wondered.

Pulling down on her small cotton *jeogori* shirt that the wind kept on lifting, exposing the skin around her waist above her skirt, Chunja comforted herself with those thoughts. She strained to swallow the scream that rolled around her tongue. Both her mind and body were frayed. Heartbroken, Chunja threw her head back and looked up at the sky.

Completely ignorant of her troubles, a brass bowl-like moon was shining in the sky and the Milky Way was flowing as well.

It was a blessed night for some, an accursed one for others. The moonlight and starlight fell on Chunja, embracing her pained, miserable, and tired body. A constellation of stars glistened in her eyes, which quietly welled up with tears.

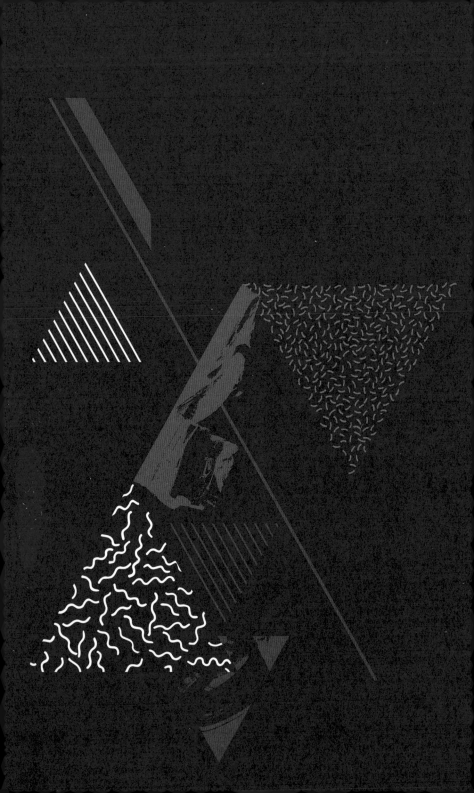

Part II

Into the Tunnel

The train continued the journey it had started that morning. The cars were rather old and dirty. Uncushioned, the wooden seats were hard, and they glistened from all the filth and grime. They bore cigarette burns here and there. The locomotive took off slowly, like a luggage-laden ox snorting with exertion. It slid out of Hoemakdong Station and picked up its pace, faster and faster. Soon, a vast open field appeared outside the windows.

Chunja stretched out her slim neck and looked outside. All she could see was an endless chain of mountains and the vast dark land underneath, occasionally marked by rivers or streams snaking across the land. She watched the continuing loop of the same scenery, but it didn't bore her.

She had no idea where the train was headed. The

scents of the breezes from the mountains and the rivers that penetrated between the window panes were signposts for her. The unfamiliar smell on her first ever rail journey was enough to make her nervous and excited.

The houses lined up along the streets were all dirty and dull-colored. But whenever they appeared, Chunja pressed her nose to the window in curiosity and looked outside with excitement and a strange sense of familiarity.

The train sometimes stopped at makeshift stations without even a station building. Even any actual stations were just buildings covered in black coal dust with wooden signboards bearing the stop's name. Every time Chunja tried to read the squiggly letters on the station signposts, the train rushed past before she was able.

When the train stopped at a station, Chinese tourists in strange attire rushed onboard. The car was full of people speaking in Chinese, a language unfamiliar to Chunja. There were Japanese people on as well. They strutted about along the narrow aisle as though they owned it.

The train reeked of dank cigarette smoke and a smell of the strong *soju* that someone must be drinking. The stench of urine emanated from the bathroom between the cars.

The train would stay only a short while at each station, and once it rattled and pulled out it would chug along the dark yellow fields, pulling dozens of cars like an old man with many children to take care of.

Then Chunja would turn her eyes back to the scenery passing by outside the window. Anyone else might have gotten sick of it, but to her the landscape outside was a continuation of dazzling displays, like a moving picture.

Suddenly, the outside turned completely dark with the sound of a gust of wind. Chunja shrank back out of fright. The train had entered a tunnel. She could hear the winds inside the quiet tunnel swirl about as the train passed by. She also smelled a whiff of acrid smoke through the window frames.

The lightbulbs on the train car ceilings blinked on. For a while, only the vibrations of the steel wheels filled the cabins. Shivering, Chunja looked up at the lightbulb above her. With a dizzying sensation of sinking into water, she felt something stirring deep inside her heart. Feeling a sense of amazement, like she was being pulled by fate, she looked at the window.

The lightbulb shone on the glass pane, which was

reflecting the inside of the train like a mirror. A girl wearing a white *jeogori* and black skirt stared back at Chunja from the window with a look of surprise on her face. Chunja scanned the blurry image on the window and started, realizing that it was her own reflection. For a long time, Chunja sat in silence, staring at her dim silhouette cast against the inky black window.

The past few days were a blur. Chunja had seen a train for the first time in her life just two days ago, and here she was riding it today.

Two days ago, Chunja went to Hoemakdong Station in the early morning. People from the church had gotten up early too, to say goodbye to Jang Mo-se, who was leaving to study theology in Pyongyang. In the street in front of the church, the pastor as well as other deacons and members stood, each giving words of encouragement.

And the choir member, Yeongsin, was there beside the departing Mo-se. Everyone's face was still puffy with sleep as it was very early in the morning, but Yeongsin was as beautiful and elegant as a swallow flying by the riverside.

Mo-se and Yeongsin hurried through the streets and

headed to the train station. After the congregants had waved goodbye and scattered, Chunja emerged from behind a utility pole along the street.

The night before, she'd confirmed Mo-se and Yeongsin's relationship in the moonlit churchyard. She felt infinitely small and worthless compared to this stunningly beautiful woman, the third daughter of a minister. On top of that, the two lovebirds' chatter that had scattered with the wind the night before continued to ring in her ears and gnaw at her heart.

Chunja spent the entire night awake. As she lay tossing and turning, the restless Gwang-ok rammed a nail into her heart with her idle chatter.

"You know, that Yeongsin, the girl who sings in the choir. She's a famed beauty in Hoemakdong. She's as beautiful as Yang Guifei, isn't she?

"And Deacon Jang! He's the Lee Mongnyong that Chunhyang has been waiting for, like in the old story. He's leaving tomorrow morning, so Yeongsin's really going to be like Chunhyang, waiting for her lover who has gone away."

"What?" asked Chunja as she sat up. "He's leaving tomorrow morning?"

"Yeah, he's taking the train," Gwang-ok chattered on in excitement. "Someone's going to be crying her eyes out."

Although Gwang-ok's words were not for her, they touched Chunja's tear ducts.

Without her realizing, a single tear escaped from the corner of her eye and trickled down her cheek. It glistened in the moonlight like a marble, and Chunja quickly wiped it from her face with her palm. It was dark, and thankfully Gwang-ok didn't notice.

Chunja felt a sudden urge to tell Gwang-ok everything. Gwang-ok was a bit scatterbrained, but nevertheless she wanted to confide in her. She wanted to grab anyone near her and ask them to listen to her.

She thought, *If I laid myself bare and showed my broken heart to someone, would this daunting feeling of emptiness subside?*

But Gwang-ok was already snoring, fast asleep.

Chunja sat alone in the darkness. She sat like a rock with her face buried in her knees all night.

As the sky turned gray at daybreak, Chunja left her aunt's house as if she were in a trance. Her eyes, red from lack of sleep, seemed anxious. Feeling stupid, she followed Mo-se and Yeongsin as though she were being drawn to them by a magnet. The couple walked quickly in front, while Chunja followed them at a good distance.

Mo-se and Yeongsin stepped into the train station. Chunja followed and looked around the building with eyes wide open like a startled chicken. It was her first time at a station and seeing a train.

The platform was full of people who had come to greet or bid farewell to others. Chunja placed her feet carefully on the platform's concrete floor as though stepping onto a stepping stone in a river. Her eyes widened when they saw the imposing train on the rails. The iron doors opened and spewed out passengers and swallowed more people as they boarded. Chunja watched the bizarre scene in curiosity.

The passengers who had stepped onto the train were scrambling to stow away their luggage. Then they pushed up the windows and stuck their heads out. Some were pulling small packages up through the windows, while others shook hands or waved goodbye to those who came to see them off. Those who were being left behind burst into tears, while those who were leaving tried hard not to cry but their eyes were reddened.

Distracted by the crowds of people on the platform, making it feel as though it were wartime, Chunja lost track of the person she'd followed. She frantically looked for Mo-se. Beside herself, she was about to burst into tears. Luckily, her eyes sought out the man she'd quietly tailed all the way to the station. The beautiful couple stood out even among a crowd.

Clad in a suit, Mo-se held a wicker suitcase. For someone who was traveling such a long way, he didn't carry much. Chunja thought he looked handsome with a ticket in one hand and the suitcase in the other.

Yeongsin followed immediately behind him like a duckling following its mother. As she was about to bid farewell to her boyfriend, she seemed apprehensive. Her head was bowed, and she kept on touching the sashes on her *jeogori*.

Before he boarded the train, Mo-se faced Yeongsin. They stood with their foreheads almost touching and whispered quietly.

Chunja stood, peeking from behind a pillar on the platform while nervously pulling on her braid.

Mo-se said, "As I told you last night, I'm taking a short

leave for my studies—I'm not leaving forever. Shouldn't you see me off with a smile?"

"I will," replied Yeongsin with a nod. But she couldn't lift her head. Tears were welled up in her big eyes. They were the exact image of a loving couple who wanted to spend every moment together and never part.

"Three years could be a long time, but it's also pretty short. And I can come visit you during school holidays."

"I know," Yeongsin kept on nodding her head.

After letting out an audible sigh that reached even Chunja's ears, Yeongsin opened her mouth.

"Focus on your studies and come back as a true minister."

Mo-se nodded his head vigorously. He gazed at her warmly. He grasped her hands tight in his. Yeongsin's cheeks reddened out of embarrassment from other people watching them, but she didn't pull away.

Holding her small hands in his, Mo-se said, "I'll pray for you while you wait for me here."

Mo-se undid the cross he wore around his neck and held it reverently in his hands.

Then he prayed in a quiet voice, "Dear God, faith is about always being alone. So people say that faith makes people lonely and solitary. And that's why folks often ask why they should go this path, and whether they should keep on walking this path. But on that solitary path you, o Lord, are with us. You walk with us, you see our tears, you know our sighs, and you hear our prayers. You wait until our waiting and our faith mature. I pray that our sisters may rely on the 'Lord's waiting' and spend their days in peace."

R-r-r-ring! The station bell rang. Chunja jumped as if she'd been burned.

At the sound of the bell, the red indicator light came on next to the rail.

Mo-se boarded the train.

The train horn blared. At its ear-blasting sound, Chunja flinched, nearly jumping out of her skin. Widening her eyes, she stared at the train that was blaring and screeching like a *dokkaebi* (Korean goblin). She watched astonished as the train, with its countless windows and percussive sounds, rolled by ed in front of her.

As the train began to depart, the platform turned chaotic. People who had come to see their loved ones off shouted and scattered like millet seeds. Everyone began to run alongside the train.

Chasing after it, people called desperate goodbyes to those aboard. Station employees in uniform walked about the platform, pulling off the people hanging onto the train.

Yeongsin covered her mouth with her hand, holding a handkerchief. Unable to hold back her tears, she sobbed loudly, and upon hearing her cry Chunja also felt her nose sting and wiped a few drops that had fallen from her watery eyes.

Why am I crying? Chunja wondered.

Even as she was being pushed and squeezed between the crowds of people, this question kept ringing in her ears. She felt that she wasn't part of this crowd of people saying farewell, someone who had no reason to be here. That thought kept her feet tethered to the spot, every time she tried to rush out and join those who were saying goodbye.

Who am I? Chunja thought. *Who am I to Mo-se? He already has someone that he loves!*

Seized by something like a sense of inferiority, Chunja couldn't step forward to bid Mo-se farewell, even though she'd followed him all the way to the station. Hiding behind a pillar on the platform and watching him as he grew distant, Chunja stood rooted to the spot. She was a meek and timid young woman who didn't have the courage to show her feelings or readily take action. She was just an innocent girl from the countryside. Chunja only hoped for a miracle: that Mo-se would see her first and wave goodbye.

Mo-se stuck his head out of the train window and waved. The cross he wore around his neck dangled. Yeongsin waved her handkerchief at him.

Still hiding behind the pillar like someone who'd committed a crime, Chunja suddenly felt that she might never have the chance to see Mo-se again. When that thought popped into her head, she rushed out from behind the pillar wearing a sorrowful and shabby face.

Mo-se's gaze, which had been fully on Yeongsin, met Chunja's eyes as she ran out from the station behind Yeongsin. His brows twitched. He squeezed his torso through the window even more. Then he yelled something.

The train horn blared at that moment, cutting off Mo-se's words. Like the frame of a painting, the window with Mo-se's image soon receded from Chunja's gaze. The long train became small like a worm until it completely disappeared into the distance.

"Mo-se…"

A whisper escaped from Yeongsin's parted lips, her eyes red with tears. It was a quiet sound, barely audible. But Chunja heard her plainly. She stared at the train tracks that stretched, enveloped in a spring haze, like two long silver snakes across the fields.

Deacon! Her heart was calling after him, just like Yeongsin's.

Sniffling, people who'd come to bid farewell began to leave the station one by one. Everyone seemed weary, having climbed out of a pit of sorrow. The platform grew empty like a field after all the radishes had been plucked. Yeongsin must also have left the platform because Chunja didn't see her anywhere.

Even though the train was long gone, an old station employee stood waving a small flag. Watching the small flag aflutter in the air, Chunja felt something like loneliness and she covered her mouth with her hands, trying to stop the tears of grief.

The platform that the train had left behind with the nasty blaring of its horn was now occupied only by lonesome silence, like a sigh. On its quiet expanse, Chunja still stood leaning against the pillar. She felt as though she would faint if she had nothing to lean on. Her heart was wild, uncertain, and desolate. She seemed to be in a daze, unable to tell whether her heart was aching, burning, or sad.

The train horn sounded, and Chunja started once again.

The train was chugging along the tracks, its rumbling mixed with the loud blaring of the horn every now and then. As it ran through the night, only the endless rattle of the train wheels sent vibrations to the passengers in the cars, which were as quiet as the grave. Noise had filled the train all day long like a day at the market, and Chunja found the silence eerie. She tried hard to get some sleep, but she'd roused again. Motion sickness came over her once more. Every time the train shook on its twin rails, her head throbbed and she felt nauseated. Looking distressed, Chunja pounded her chest with her fist.

"Are you okay?" asked Gwang-ok.

Factory Girl Recruitment

"You wench, where have you been this late at night!"

The moment Chunja returned with her eyes still red, her aunt yelled at her. Her voice sounded so much like her mother's that she jumped. For a second, she thought she was back at home in Deer Valley instead of at her aunt's house in Hoemakdong.

Her yelling yanked Chunja back to reality. Once again, she felt the burden of worries on her shoulder like a heavy rock placed on top of pickled cucumbers. It had been two days since she arrived at her aunt's house, but her mother's sister showed no sign of being willing to lend her money. She didn't even give Chunja enough food to eat— the only thing she did was to hint at her to leave. When doing the dishes, she clattered the utensils loudly, and she badmouthed Chunja, pretending to talk about the guests of her inn while saying that some people couldn't take a hint.

Yet even as her face burned with shame, Chunja stubbornly remained at her aunt's house. No matter the poor reception she received there, she was even more worried about heading home to Deer Valley empty-handed. She didn't even want to imagine what would happen if she returned with nothing to her mom, who, forced to raise her daughter all by herself, had turned cranky and mean at some point like a pregnant tigress.

And the harvest had been woeful last year. During the rice planting time, the weather was awfully dry, and then it poured with rain in the summer, sweeping away several houses by the riverbank. The crop yield was barely over half the average. As a result, the cruel barley hump came early this spring.

Kkeutsun's stomach was completely empty, and her angry outbursts worsened like acute indigestion. Chunja's anxiety at having to face her mother even dried all the tears she had been shedding for her unrequited love.

On that day, Chunja stood in the alley in front of her aunt's inn, scratching a hole in the ground with the tip of her shoe. She was planning to tough it out and keep pestering her aunt for money. Yet still daunted at the prospect of having to face the older woman who was as scary as her mother and who waited inside, Chunja couldn't step into the house.

As she stood hesitating in the alley, someone called out to her.

"Oh, what a pretty face!"

A woman dressed in fancy clothing walked toward Chunja, her heels clicking and clacking on the paved street. She started talking to Chunja from afar. With high cheekbones and a pointy chin, she was a woman in her forties with her face powdered white, as though she'd covered herself in lime powder. Clad in a skirt suit with a purse in her hand, she walked over, swinging her hips from side to side. But above all, the waves of her curly, permed hair caught Chunja's eyes. The girl fidgeted with her braided hair timidly.

The woman approached Chunja with the tips of her heels noisily tapping on the ground. Chunja caught a strong whiff of perfume. Holding tightly onto reality, she stared squarely at the woman's face that seemed to shine like the sun.

"You look clever. Honey, would you be interested in working at a nice factory by any chance?"

"Who… are you, ma'am?" asked Chunja, pulling herself out of a stupor caused by the strong scent of the woman's perfume. Chunja was confused, like a hotel guest who'd entered the wrong room.

"I'm from Bin-gang Textile Factory in Bongcheon (Shenyang)."

After introducing herself, she asked Chunja, "Do you know how to read?"

"Yes, a bit…" answered Chunja shyly, still fidgeting with her hair.

The woman pulled out a small piece of paper from her purse and held it out to Chunja. She pointed her index finger at the words on it. Her fingernails were polished bright red. Chunja stared at the crimson nails, intrigued. They were much more colorful than her fingernails had been that time she'd dyed them with garden balsams for fun.

Having narrowly avoided remaining illiterate by attending the night school, Chunja read the words the woman was pointing at. It was as if her red fingernail was luring her and leading her, like a shaman summoning her soul.

As if under hypnosis, Chunja read the words without realizing that she was talking out loud.

"The Bin-gang Textile Company is recruiting more women to increase its business. Any woman between the ages of eighteen and twenty-five who is healthy can apply. Preference given to women who are fluent in Japanese. Monthly wage is fifty won. Anyone who wishes is welcome to apply."

"Oh, *jouzu*! (you're good!)" the woman uttered in Japanese. She then switched to Korean again and said, "Good job. Pretty and you even know how to read."

Chunja felt her cheeks blush at the woman's sweet talk. The woman explained the advertisement that Chunja had just read in plain words. She said that the Bin-gang Textile Company, established by a trading firm in Japan, had acquired a fabric mill in Seoul and was expanding its business to Manchuria, and it was recruiting many girls to work there.

"Where else would you find a more enticing opportunity?" The fancy words flowed out from between the woman's red lips. Her voice was loud and clear, and she was acting rather bold.

Chunja stared agape as the woman's lips poured out impressive talk without pause; it was as though she were watching a magician giving an elaborate performance.

"Is a pretty girl like you going to spend the rest of your life digging around in the dirt with your pretty hands? You have to go to the city, become a factory girl, and have a bright life. Just go and take a look. You'll see that it's a paradise."

Even as she spoke on and on, her eyes never left Chunja's body. Chunja blushed in embarrassment as the woman continued to scan Chunja up and down without reservation.

"If you agree to work at the factory, you'll receive fifty won per month, six hundred won total a year. So if you work there for a few years, you'll be free from wretched poverty, right? And you could even marry someone nice."

Chunja stood, still a bit confused, and the woman said, "If you agree to come, you'll get an advance of ten won."

The woman studied Chunja's face as she spoke. Chunja's sunken eyes widened and tensed in surprise.

"What? An advance?"

Her eyes shone like a child's upon finding a piece of candy. The huge sum of six hundred won a year sounded completely unreal to Chunja. She couldn't tell how much money that would mean and she'd never wished to have so much. But the advance of ten won lifted her heart like the spring wind that rustled her skirt.

The woman pulled out a ten-won bill as if to prove that her statement was true. Chunja's eyes were focused on the pinkish bill. The amount of money that her mother had asked her to borrow from her aunt was exactly ten won. It would take Chunja and her mother a year of back-breaking labor to pay Chunja's aunt back the following autumn. But if she went to work at the textile factory, she would earn even more than that.

Chunja licked her rough, dry lips.

"Okay. I'm in."

The reply came. But it wasn't from Chunja's lips. It came from behind her.

It was Gwang-ok. Gwang-ok had snuck up behind her at some point and answered even before Chunja, giving into her impetuous nature. Then she grinned wide at Chunja, sticking out her tongue in embarrassment.

Having gained an ally, Chunja squared her shrugged shoulders. She nodded alongside Gwang-ok and cleared her throat before saying, "Yes, I will go."

The woman smiled, raising her already high cheekbones even higher.

After several days on the train, they finally disembarked. When they'd boarded they felt excited and curious to ride the rails for the first time in their lives, but staying on it for days at a time proved to be a rather difficult task.

Chunja and Gwang-ok leaned against each other like pieces of luggage and spent days and nights half-awake, enduring the torment of the train's clattering and rattling. The announcement that they'd soon be getting off jolted them awake. They yelled for joy on the inside, thankful that this seemingly unending, boring journey was at an end.

Just as she was about to get off the train, Chunja halted abruptly before putting her foot down on the steps. The outside was covered in a dense morning fog. The fog was laid so thick that she couldn't see a few steps ahead of her, and fear blanketed her like a piece of white cloth.

"Why are you just standing there? Get off, quick!"

The recruiter woman shoved her from behind. Her hands were strong. Chunja nearly fell headlong on the ground.

"How will you make money if you dawdle like this?"

Grumbling, the woman with high cheekbones rushed other girls off the train. Under her direction, Chunja was on the platform.

There had been many girls on the train about Chunja and Gwang-ok's age, all of them recruited to work at the textile factory. They were from Hoemakdong, Yongdeurechon, Gukjaga (Yanji), and Hoeryeong.

"I'm Sunhwa," a tall girl from Gukjaga introduced herself first.

"I'm Hyesuk. I'm from Yongdeurechon."

She was scrawny like a shrike, so thin that a strong hug might snap her in two.

"I'm from Hoeryeong. My name is Ok. *Unni* (older sisters), I look forward to working with you and hope to learn from you."

The girl from Hoeryeong spoke with a North Korean accent, and she was only about thirteen or fourteen with pure pitch-black irises. Her clear and innocent eyes were like those of a small child. And perhaps that was why they also looked so reckless.

196

"Aw, you're just a baby," said Gwang-ok, clicking her tongue. "How did you even learn about this opportunity?"

The train entered a tunnel, almost as though it were sucked into it. Chunja could see Gwang-ok smiling, exposing her white teeth in the darkness. Chunja suffered from motion sickness aboard the train, but Gwang-ok was completely fine. Her eyes sparkled with excitement that she seemed unable to hide. The eyes of all those who were wearing simple and shabby clothing like Gwang-ok were full of expectations. Having introduced themselves to others, some seemed to have made friends, as there were occasional giggles.

As the train rolled on, the woman with high cheekbones introduced herself, saying, "I'm a recruiter from Japan for the Bin-gang Textile Company."

"Huh?" Chunja widened her eyes. "She's from Walbon?"

Chunja was surprised that the woman spoke fluent Korean and remembered that she'd occasionally exclaimed or mumbled something in Japanese.

"The textile company, it must be run by Japanese people," Gwang-ok whispered into Chunja's ear.

Once again, the train entered a tunnel. They didn't know how many tunnels they'd passed through. At first, they counted every single one out of fascination, but after ten of them, Chunja and Gwang-ok stopped their tally. Like a serpent slithering out of a bottomless pit on its way to become a dragon, the train passed through one tunnel after the other.

Every time the train went through the mouth of a tunnel, Chunja was enveloped by groundless fear. She didn't like the pitch-black, and she didn't like the lightbulbs that lit up like someone opening their eyes wide and glaring at her. She also didn't want to see the reflection of herself and others like her in the train window, who looked exhausted from the long ride.

As anxiety inundated her, she felt an urge to pee. Chunja thought that it was simply unimaginable to go to the bathroom on a moving train. Gwang-ok went several times, but Chunja decided to hold it. Only when she couldn't hold it any longer because her bladder felt like it would burst any second did she head to the toilet. Yet her steps were reluctant, as if she were heading to a lion's den.

The moment she entered the bathroom that was smaller than an old tobacco drying hut, Chunja froze.

There was a hole on the floor, and she could see the pebbles and railroad ties passing rapidly by.

"Oh my goodness!" Chunja exclaimed, as if she'd stepped on a snake, and ran out of the bathroom.

And at that moment, her skirt was soaked. Chunja stood rooted to the spot in the boxlike space in between train cars. The train sounded louder and rattled even more. But she couldn't possibly leave.

Back when she'd wet the bed as a child, her mother would place a winnowing tray upside down upon her head and send her next door to ask for salt. It was so embarrassing that Chunja used to cry at the top of her lungs at the straw by the gate of their neighbor's house with the winnowing tray on her head.

Just as she had then, she felt ashamed, as if she'd become the center of the entire world's attention. If she had a winnowing tray now, she would have used it to cover her face. Blaming someone she didn't even know for this situation she was in, Chunja wrung the wet part of her skirt as she thought, *I promised myself I would wear it nicely because auntie gave these clothes to me…*

The skirt and *jeogori* were covered in lint balls and discolored here and there, but they were certainly more wearable than the ones that Chunja had had on, which were little better than rags. Chunja's eyes welled up with tears out of embarrassment and anxiety, but they soon dried.

"No, even if this is hard, I mustn't cry. I'll be making money from now on…"

Muttering to herself, Chunja held the wet end of her skirt in her hand and let her body rock with the rattling of the train. Once again, the train rushed headlong into a tunnel without hesitation.

The girls who had followed the recruiter woman with high cheekbones and had spent days and nights eating and sleeping on the train got off one by one. At a glance, there were about twenty or so girls who looked about as shabby as Chunja did. Weary from the journey, they seemed a bit grubby or weak.

Chunja also felt overcome with extreme fatigue and weak knees, having spent several days dealing with the train's constant rocking. She was so tired that the bluish semicircles under her eyes seemed particularly dark and conspicuous. But their sweet fantasies about their futures made everyone forget their fatigue.

The day before she left, when Chunja took out the money she'd received as an advance—the ten-won bill that she'd folded many times and held tightly in her hand—her aunt looked startled. Chunja told her about taking a job at a factory and asked her to do all she could to send the money to her mom in Deer Valley. Her aunt gazed at Chunja with mixed feelings. She muttered to herself, "Poverty is the enemy."

Then recalling how inhospitable she'd been to Chunja until then, she quietly began to speak.

"Don't be mad at me for being so rough. The inn doesn't make as much money as you think, you know. I want to help, but we really don't get a lot of customers, and my husband gets annoyed at me for lending money…"

She grasped Chunja's hand as if to say sorry. Then she pulled up the train of her skirt to dab the corners of her eyes.

"I'll make sure to take this money to Deer Valley, so don't worry. It's been a while since I've seen *unni*, anyway."

As though that wasn't enough, Chunja's aunt also gave

her a set of *jeogori* and skirt. She said she'd only worn them a few times because she cherished them. Chunja's mouth widened into a smile at the very first present she'd ever received in her life. All the animosity she'd felt toward her aunt melted away like snow.

But when Gwang-ok grew excited and antsy as she explained that she wanted to join Chunja, Chunja's aunt flatly dismissed the idea. Throwing a glance at Chunja, she scolded Gwang-ok in a low voice, "Stupid girl! You don't even know what kind of terrible place that is and you're dying to go?"

The next day, Chunja headed to the train station without anyone seeing her off. She'd been told to come to the station early in the morning. The train fare was already paid for, the woman had said. It was her second time at the train station, but it still felt unfamiliar and scary to Chunja.

As she hurried around the platform, looking for the stylish woman who had recruited her, someone suddenly clutched her shoulders. Chunja turned around and saw Gwang-ok.

"You followed me here?" asked Chunja in surprise.

"Did your mom let you come?"

"I snuck out!" said Gwang-ok with a giggle.

"No, no. Go home quick."

Chunja turned her around, nudging her to head on back home, but Gwang-ok grasped Chunja's hands and argued, "But when I make a lot of money and return home, my mom will say, 'My daughter's such a good daughter,' and she'll be happy."

"No. Go on home now. If you don't, auntie will think that I talked you into coming with me. Go home, quick. Go on!"

Watching Chunja try and stop her, Gwang-ok suddenly put on a serious face and said, "To tell you the truth, my mom's having a hard time because our inn's not really doing well. She's been saying that we should just give up, but then it's not bad enough to just give it away so she can't. And no one else wants to take it over either. So we can't do anything right now. But if I make a fortune and send it to her, she'd be able to get the inn up and running again."

Gwang-ok had always seemed like a simple and silly girl, so Chunja stared, opening and closing her mouth, as Gwang-ok made a clear and considerate statement for the first time. She couldn't possibly stop Gwang-ok from coming. So the two of them boarded the train together.

Now that she was going to work at a factory, if she spent a few years working hard, Chunja thought that she'd be able to get away from the terrible poverty that had turned her mom into a mean shrew and the object of the entire village's sad gazes. And she also thought that it would help erase the pain of her unrequited love for the man who'd up and left Deer Valley and even Hoemakdong. When her thoughts went there, Chunja followed closely behind all the other girls, afraid that she might be left behind, and gave her full attention to the recruiter woman's words.

The place where the young women disembarked was a shabby temporary station. There was no building or station employee. Only the picket spiked into the ground next to the rails, the sign standing erect amidst thick fog, seemed to indicate that this was also a station. Chunja looked hard at the sign to figure out where they were. The sign was written in Chinese. She recognized one of the characters—"石" meaning "rock." She didn't know the rest. She had no idea how far she'd come from her hometown or where this place was.

Suddenly something black that had sat huddled on the sign took off and flew into the sky. Chunja jumped with fright.

The crow cawed in a harsh, shrill tone as it tore through the fog above Chunja's head. At the bird's plaintive cry, Chunja shuddered once again.

"Ptui!" Gwang-ok spat on the ground three times at the portent of bad luck.

"An unlucky crow so early in the morning. Shoo! Shoo!"

Gwang-ok flailed her arms as though she herself were trying to fly to chase away the crow. A few other girls followed suit and spat on the ground.

"Where are we?" Sunhwa, the girl from Gukjaga, asked the recruiter woman. Her permed hair was now undone and looking frizzy as if she had a woven basket on her head, the woman didn't answer her question.

"Are we nearly there yet? Where are we going?"

Hyesuk from Yongdeurechon also asked, but there was no reply from the woman. Her eyes were shut, as if she were refusing to give them an answer. She rummaged through her purse and took something out. It was a pack of cigarettes. She pulled out a cigarette. She stuck it between her lips and lit it with a click of her lighter. It was the first time she'd seen a woman smoke, so Chunja stared at the unusual sight. Not caring at all about what the girls were thinking, the recruiter smoked her cigarette in silence. The smoke rose and mingled with the fog.

Then the woman let out a long yawn. Chunja noticed that the top of her tongue was coated white. The image of a stylish and beautiful city woman that she'd seen a few days prior vanished right before Chunja's eyes like so much cigarette smoke.

"Where in the world are we?" Gwang-ok asked loudly, no longer able to keep herself still.

The woman snapped her head around.

"Did you swallow a crow whole?" She barked irritably. "Why are you yelling?"

With her makeup partly erased, her face looked blue.

"But where are we? We're only asking if we're there yet." Sunhwa from Gukjaga asked once again.

The woman answered in a voice as cold as the early morning air, "We still have a long way to go. You'll know when you get there."

It was early summer, but there was no hint of warmth in the early morning air. Even the weather was gloomy, and a chill hung in the air at the station. The morning fog clung to the body like silk that had been soaked in cold water. The chilly air penetrated Chunja's frayed *jeogori*. Hugging a small sack of her possessions, Chunja shuddered in the cold. Gwang-ok's lips were blue from the cold as well. Chunja walked over and hugged her tight. The two of them huddled together and warmed each other with the heat of their bodies.

At that moment, a truck rattled and lurched into the temporary station. It was early morning and very foggy, so the truck had its headlights on. Flashing its big headlights and lurching forward, the vehicle looked like a mad ox. Raging like a beast, the truck approached the girls at full speed almost as if to run them over, and the girls screamed.

Then it stopped abruptly in front of them, kicking up a dust storm. Someone hopped down from the driver's seat. Coughing from the dust, Chunja looked at the driver. He was a rugged man. But there was something strange about his clothes. Clad in a khaki cap and uniform, he was dressed like a soldier. Dust lined the seams on the shoulders of his military uniform, creating gray lines.

The recruiter woman quickly discarded her cigarette and approached the man in hurried steps. The woman was all smiles, but the man seemed indifferent. Soon the woman returned to the girls.

"You've all had a difficult journey on the train, but you still have a long way to go. Now, you should follow him and get on the truck."

The girls hesitated. A tarp covered the truck's cargo area, and like the man's uniform it was khaki. Overwhelmed by the truck's ghastly, beastlike appearance, the girls dithered.

"*Sassato nore* (stop wasting time and get on)!" The man in khaki yelled at the girls, pointing to the cargo area of the truck.

Unable to understand him, the girls all turned their heads and looked at the recruiter woman.

"Get on the truck!" the woman yelled. It was an irritated shriek. Her face had completely transformed, and she began pushing the girls frantically toward the truck. Her eyes were full of spite as she rushed the girls to board.

Chunja floundered, having difficulty climbing up the

high truck. The woman's rough smack landed on her back.

"Stop dawdling, you wenches!"

A foul smell wafted from her lips that were now free of lipstick. Chunja thought that the woman resembled a demon, her face with its smudged makeup.

The recruiter's complete about-face confused her. She struggled to get over the truck's tailgate and into the cargo area, which seemed as high as a wall. Gwang-ok got on the truck first and held out her hand to Chunja. With arms as weak as wet tissue, Chunja grasped Gwang-ok's wrist and finally managed to climb aboard the truck.

All the girls climbed into the truck with the desperation of people hanging onto a cliff. The inside was akin to an abandoned mine. A military blanket with a slight sheen from grime was being used to cover the rear of the truck. When all the girls had climbed aboard, the blanket covered the opening like a flap.

Darkness descended on the girls as though someone had thrown blank ink everywhere. The inside of the truck was pitch black, making it difficult to see even the people sitting close by. Just like all the other girls, Chunja sat down on the floor of the truck. Coldness shot up through her buttocks. Chunja jumped, as if she'd been stabbed by the spike of a gimlet. But the truck rattled sideways, making her slump back down again.

When the truck moved, it caused a corner of the blanket to lift. Chunja looked outside through the gap. She could see the recruiter woman at the station. In the fog, she was following the truck with her eyes shaded dark with makeup. She seemed to be smiling, her cheekbones high.

"Oh, is that woman not coming with us?" The girl from Yongdeurechon—Hyesuk—asked in surprise.

"Where are we going?"

A few of the girls asked the same question out loud, but there was no one to give an answer. A sense of extreme fear fell over the girls. A cloud of dirt trailed the truck like a fog. The reeling of the vehicle only added to their anxiety. In the lurching cargo section, the girls bounced like balls. Holding each other's hands, they were awkwardly jostled around, unable to sit or stand.

The blanket that functioned like a back door began to flap in the wind. The cold air slashed at their skin. A whirl of wind blew into the truck, stirring the girls' clothes and ruffling their hair. Chunja huddled, arching her back forward like a bow, to try and avoid the wind that was coming at her with sharp claws. Wind blew into her *jeogori*, swelling it up like a balloon. Pulling her top down, Chunja kept on looking outside. Through the flapping blanket, she gazed vaguely at the hazy, foggy scenery.

After hours of being rocked and buffeted around on the truck like children being beaten by an angry stepfather, the vehicle finally came to a stop. The blanket was rolled up, and the same rugged man appeared.

"*Hayaku oriro* (get off quickly)!" the man barked ferociously.

The girls guessed what the man was telling them to do. Halting and stumbling, they began to get off the truck. A few girls squatted down on the ground and vomited as soon as they alighted. The contents of their stomachs spurted out of their mouths and splattered on the trains of their skirts. Some tried to cover their mouths and head to a corner somewhere, but they could only take a few steps before they stopped and retched.

Chunja's reaction was the most severe. Motion sickness from the train and now the bumpy truck ride made her heave until tears came from her eyes. With one hand pressed against her chest, she opened and closed her mouth like a fish gasping for breath. Yet even as she did so, she looked around the surroundings with tears in her eyes. They were surrounded by a huge wall. On both sides of the crude wooden gate were two soldiers facing each other. The rifles in their hands made the girls' hearts sink. One of the soldiers on guard looked toward the girls like a heron eyeing fish in shallow waters. Disconcerted by his penetrating gaze, Chunja turned her head.

"She said it was a textile factory, but is this place a munitions factory?" mumbled Sunhwa.

"Looks like it," said Gwang-ok. "Why are soldiers guarding a factory of all places?"

In front of them was a building with perpendicular wings on both sides that made it look like a school. Confused, as though she'd just been jolted awake from a dream, Chunja looked around with her sunken eyes.

"*Tsuite koi* (follow me)!" the man in military uniform yelled again. His voice was harsh and screeching, like a glass shard slashing its hearers to pieces.

At his shrill voice, the girls tensed and formed a line, as if they'd been bound with a rope. A string of girls, all similarly wearing white *jeogori* and black skirts and sporting long braids that reached down to their buttocks, walked into the building one after another.

There was a sign on the door to the building. The words written with a brush on the wooden sign said: Army Comfort Station.

Khaki-Colored Terror

The girls walked into a huge auditorium. A feeling of uneasiness came over them, making them feel faint. Standing shoulder to shoulder, some hugging one another, they stood in a tight group and whispered words that didn't really need to be said into each other's ears.

Heavy unease also hung like the dense morning fog about Chunja's shoulders. Unable to shake off the nebulous fear that enveloped her, she fumbled for and grasped Gwang-ok's hand. She hunched her shoulders without realizing.

Gwang-ok was just as scared. Her wavering eyes darted aimlessly from side to side.

Where are we? What are we supposed to do here? Those questions alone ran through their heads. Eventually, there was a sound from the door. Led by the rugged man who'd driven the girls in the truck, two people entered the auditorium.

The first was a man with a bigger head and broader shoulders than the rugged driver. He had a muscular torso and a thick, short neck. The soldier's cap looked small on his head, with its shaved sides. It made him look dull and callous. He was also wearing a military uniform and, unlike the driver, had stars on his epaulettes. The corpulent, brutish man put his hands on his hips by his belt and looked around at the girls.

The second new person to enter the auditorium was a woman. She was fully dressed in Japanese attire, namely a blue *wafuku*. Wearing a pair of *tabi* socks and wooden *geta* on her feet, she walked in with quite a loud click-clack noise. All the girls stared at the woman in the colorful dress standing among the soldiers clad in khaki uniforms. It was early in the morning still, but her face was plastered with makeup, forming a white mask that made it difficult to tell her expression. The woman, who seemed to be in her forties, walked straight toward the girls. Every time she took a step, her *geta* clacked loudly, piercing everyone's ears. The noise grated on the nerves of the already tense girls.

The click and clack of her *geta* stopped in front of
Chunja. The woman's gaze remained on her lean face and
slim figure. She stared at Chunja for a while. Embarrassed
by her unabashed stare, Chunja fidgeted with the collar of
her *jeogori*.

"*Ara, kireine* (oh, how pretty)!" the woman said.
Something like a smile appeared on her mask-like face for
a moment before it disappeared.

Sturdy-looking soldiers stepped up toward the girls.
Under the brim of their caps pulled down low, they
glowered at the girls one by one. Overcome with fear for
no particular reason, the girls crouched their shoulders.
They couldn't see the men's eyes under the caps, but their
gazes were intense.

The recruiter woman had told them she was fixing
them up with a good job, but now that they were
here, people were treating them rudely, as if they were
criminals. Nevertheless, assuming that this was just part
of the usual process, the girls complied.

After lashing them with a venomous gaze, the soldier
who entered the auditorium with the driver began to
speak. He held up his index finger and enunciated every
word. Blue veins showed on his short, stubby finger.

"My name is Nakamura Nobuyuki, and I am the officer in charge of these troops."

The girls couldn't understand what he was saying, but the tone of his voice was haughty. The woman in *wafuku* translated his Japanese into fluent Korean. After introducing himself, Officer Nobuyuki pointed to the woman who was translating his words.

"And this is Ms. Shiono Minami, who joined the Women's Patriotic Unit and came all the way here to China for our victory in this great war."

The woman smiled as she interpreted, "I'm Shiono Minami. From now on, you girls can just call me *okaasan*. It means mother."

"Mother?" the girls whispered.

Despite her gentle smile and exhortation to call her by a rather warm appellation, the girls didn't feel any kindness from her guileful mask-like face. They eyed the woman rather warily. Dressed in a gorgeous *wafuku* and wearing full makeup so early in the morning, she seemed dubious—her identity unclear like the dense fog outside.

"For convenience, we will assign a number to each of you."

The woman—Shiono—handed a number tag to every

girl. The wooden tags had numbers etched in black ink. Chunja was number 13. By her side, Gwang-ok held up her tag. She smiled, flashing the tag at Chunja. Silly Gwang-ok was number 12.

"I'm number 14. I think I'm after you, *unni*."

Ok, the young girl from Hoeryeong, approached Chunja and showed her tag. Then she smiled timidly. In response, Chunja held up her tag and smiled as well. But the smiles they exchanged were half-hearted.

After the number tags, each girl was handed a small pouch. On the khaki-colored pouch, akin to one that Buddhist monks carried to ask for donations, were the words "Advance First" in Chinese characters.

"What does it say on this tiny pouch?"

"Something first, I think?"

The girls asked each other about the text.

Giving into her curiosity, Gwang-ok opened her pouch and took out its contents.

"Huh? What is this?"

Gwang-ok looked perplexed as she held up a small rubber sac. The same thing was in Chunja's pouch. Finding the slippery texture of the rubber off-putting, Chunja frowned.

Shiono laughed out loud. Her short and sudden laugher startled the others.

"You don't know what that is?" she asked amusingly. "It's called *sakku*."

"Huh?"

All the girls' eyes landed on Shiono.

"This is called *sakku*, Shiono explained as she giggled. "It prevents you from getting pregnant. Before you get to work, you must put this on the men."

As if to demonstrate, Shiono inserted her thumb into the rubber sac.

The girls let their heads drop, stunned. Ok flinched as if she'd touched a cockroach, and the pouch fell from her hand.

Shiono picked it up and handed it back to her. Then she said to the girl, who seemed about to burst into tears, "This is like your locker. Do not throw it away recklessly. It's important that you have it and use it every day."

Chunja was completely befuddled. She couldn't understand what the woman in her fancy *wafuku* was telling them. Suddenly the khaki pouch in her hand containing a rubber with a mysterious purpose felt heavy, as if it were full of rocks.

"What is it?" asked Hwasun from Gukjaga. "What is it that we have to do?"

Shiono laughed again and quietly said, "It's nothing difficult. Any woman can do it."

"So what is it?" The girls asked. There was a sense of urgency to their question.

Giving them a serious look, Shiono said, "What you have to do now is…" Mid-sentence, she turned to look at the sturdy military officer standing next to her and continued, "to serve the soldiers of the Great Empire of Japan. You are to comfort the tired bodies of the men who are dedicating themselves to the Greater East Asia War."

Silence filled the auditorium. None of the girls spoke, as though they'd been grabbed by their hair and pulled headlong under water. Some girls had turned pale in shock as if they'd been drenched in ice cold water.

"What?" Hwasun screamed, breaking the stifling silence.

"We were recruited to work at a factory. What are you talking about?"

"That's right. We came to work at a factory."

The girls seethed and protested. Feeling dazed, like this was all a dream, Chunja also raised her voice, "Right!

We came to work at a factory. At a textile factory."

But pretending not to hear them, Shiono continued, "Your work here is more important than that of factory girls. You are here to do your duty for the Greater East Asia Empire. It is something that all women have to do at some point. So isn't it great that you can boost the morale of the soldiers and make money at the same time?"

"How can you say that?"

"What on earth is that woman saying?"

The girls shouted in panic.

"*Yakamashii* (quiet)! *Shizukani shiro* (shut up)!"

Nobuyuki shouted in a grating voice. The corners of his eyes crinkled under the brim of his cap. As if the tone of his voice were contagious, Shiono's soft and gentle voice changed. Her voice rose higher above those of the girls. In a harsh tone like fingernails on a chalkboard, she said, "It doesn't matter if you didn't know this was where you were coming. We already bought you for five hundred won per head. On top of that, we paid a tip to the recruiters."

The image of the woman with high cheekbones popped up in Chunja's head and soon vanished.

"It's already water under a bridge," Shiono said. "Whether you want to or not, this is what you are here to do."

What was this ridiculous nonsense? Chunja thought. The woman had said that she'd help Chunja escape poverty, and she'd even given her an advance… but now that Chunja was here after a long journey, she realized she was standing in a lion's den.

Chunja placed her hands on her chest. Her heart was pounding, and she felt breathless, as if her chest was made of aluminum foil and was being crumpled up. Her heart felt like it was going to burst.

"But we came here thinking we would be working at a factory. We can do any kind of work no matter how hard, so long as it's not this."

The girls pleaded, still stunned and appalled.

"What? You want to do something else? Like what?"

Shiono crossed her arms. In response to the girls' words, she flatly said, "This is the only work available here."

"What the hell!" screams erupted from here and there.

"This is absurd! We want to go home."

"Right. This was just a silly dream. We want to go back."

"Let's forget about this factory girl recruitment. We

want to go home."

The girls heaved in anxiety as they spoke up. Ok from Hoeryeong stood pouting and suddenly burst into tears.

Shiono hovered around the girls. Over the sound of her clacking *geta*, she said, "Fine. You can leave. But if you want to leave…"

She held out her hand, palm up, toward the girls.

"Give me five hundred won now. Give me the money we paid to bring you here."

At her unfair demand, the girls were at a loss for words. They only opened and closed their mouths like fish thrown on the ground, trying to catch a breath.

When there seemed to be a lull among them, Shiono began to chatter away.

"Just be quiet for a moment and listen to your *okaasan*. Filial piety is the most important thing to you Korean girls, and if you just bear with it a little and work here, you'll be able to pay the five hundred won back to us and make even more money to send to your parents."

Shiono coaxed and cajoled the girls in a gentle voice. Then suddenly her gentle voice jumped into a high-pitched screech as though someone had pinched her thigh.

"And how would you even go anywhere else? You can try running away. But we're hundreds of miles from your hometowns. And this is a military camp. You may have walked in freely, but walking out of here is not going to be easy."

Having tossed out those stiff words, Shiono glanced at the gate. The girls followed her gaze. Soldiers holding rifles had arrived at the gate and stood guarding it. They were all wearing khaki-colored uniforms, and their faces were solemn like the statues of gatekeepers at Buddhist temples.

Everything was khaki—the soldiers' caps, their uniforms, shoes, the truck that the girls had been on, the building, the window frames in the auditorium, and even the wooden floor. Chunja had never felt so terrified by the color khaki. The khaki-colored terror had already covered all the girls, like green dye spilt on a white *jeogori*. That fear had spread on their faces. Stunned, they blankly stared at Shiono's lips as she chattered on enthusiastically.

"This is a military camp in the middle of nowhere. Even if you can get out of this place, you'll be eaten by herds of wild dogs or wolves."

After spitting out such threats, Shiono suddenly

laughed, her laugh sounding like a slap in the face.

"But if you still want to go, I won't stop you," she spoke harshly. "I have nothing to lose. I'll just go to your parents and get the five hundred won back. And we'll order them to repay us for the food you ate, your train fare, and our trouble in double."

Chunja swallowed hard. Her mind went blank like an empty piece of paper.

The corpulent officer stepped forward.

"Now I will tell you the rules of the Army Entertainment Center. Listen closely and observe these rules."

Completely ignoring how the girls were feeling, the Japanese officer explained the regulations, and Shiono parroted his words to the girls in Korean.

"This comfort station is for the soldiers and civilians attached to the army and does not permit entry to the general public. Locals cannot come here.

"Soldiers who enter this comfort station will have a ticket. The ticket is only valid for that day.

"The price of the ticket will be two won for non-commissioned officers and infantry soldiers, two *won* and two *jeon* for army civilians, and three won for commissioned officers. Make sure to remember all of this. As soon as a soldier enters the room, you must take his ticket. You have the right to refuse service to those who don't have tickets.

"You will spend no more than twenty minutes with each soldier. One hour for officers. Allowing a soldier to stay overnight is strictly prohibited.

"The service women cannot leave the army comfort station at will. You are prohibited from taking walks or wandering around outside the walls of the comfort station."

Nobuyuki held up his head and glared at the girls with his twitchy eyes. Visible from under the brim of his cap, they shone both black and blue. Once more he held up his short, stubby forefinger with snaking blue veins and enunciated every word. Shiono's voice also rose, swayed by the jerky movements of his finger.

"If you serve the warriors of His Majesty the Emperor with the attitude of sacrificing yourselves for the public good, you will be generously compensated. But if you think to do otherwise, the outcome will be unimaginable."

Chunja felt an eerie chill creep up her spine to the top of her head. It made her skin crawl. The girls were lined up and led to the next place.

Shiono in her blue *wafuku* stood at the front of the line, and when the girls hesitated, the rough-looking officer Nobuyuki roared at them to hurry.

"*Hayaku, hayaku!*"

The girls looked browbeaten as they exited the auditorium. Shiono's face was taut and dull, unlike her stylish *wafuku*, and Nobuyuki was scowling like hell's gatekeeper. He furrowed his brow and fiercely rolled his eyes. They herded the girls together and shepherded them like goats. Irritated voices pommeled the girls' ears like roaring thunder.

A small hand touched Chunja's hand. Chunja turned around. It was Ok from Hoeryeong.

"*Unni*, where are we going now?" she asked in a voice barely louder than the buzz of a mosquito. Her eyes were sunken like those of a frightened puppy.

Looking down at her in mournful silence, Chunja shook her head from side to side. She didn't know where they were going or what was going to happen to them. No one knew.

Shiono's feet stopped in front of a room at the east end of the hall. The entrance to the room was covered with a sheet of white cloth. The cloth was stained with grime.

The girls all stared at Shiono.

"This is the dispensary," Shiono said with a dramatic expression on her face. "We will take care of your health, so now you will undergo a medical examination."

The white curtain rustled in the wind. A pungent smell wafted on the air from inside the room. Chunja flared her nostrils without realizing. When the white curtain rolled up in the wind, she cocked her head to the side and looked inside. There were a few people waiting within.

"Now, go in two at a time."

Shiono pointed at two girls in order. First up were Gwang-ok and Hyesuk from Yongdeurechon. But within a few minutes of entering the room, the curtain flapped and Gwang-ok bolted out. Enveloped in the smell of antiseptic, she ran for it, rejecting the dispensary staff with all the strength she had.

"I won't!" she screamed. "I won't do it!"

Someone in a white gown rushed out after her, yelling, "*Matte, kochi koi* (stop, come here)!"

The person was wearing a white gown, but the military cap suggested that they were a medical officer. Blocking Gwang-ok as she rushed out of the dispensary, Nobuyuki grabbed her by the collar.

"*Chikushou* (you savage)!"

He smacked Gwang-ok's cheeks mercilessly.

"Stupid girl, have you gone mad from joy just because they're giving you a free medical exam?" Shiono prattled mockingly beside her.

The medic in the white gown grabbed Gwang-ok by her arm and dragged her back into the room. A low scream seemed to come from the inside. Moments later, Hyesuk came out, followed by Gwang-ok. They both waddled out, their legs spread apart. Struggling to walk, Gwang-ok looked over at Chunja. Her eyes were full of something like shock and shame. When the two of them returned to the line of girls, they stood leaning against each other.

The tall girl from Gukjaga named Sunhwa and Chunja were called next. As if she were pushing aside tree branches and entering a cave, Chunja pushed the curtain aside and reluctantly stepped into the room. A pungent smell of antiseptic stung her nose. The strong smell lashed at her, causing her to cover her nose and mouth with her hand. There were two beds in the room, and there were several people clad in white gowns and masks standing by them.

White curtain, white gown, white mask, white gloves… For a moment the white color looked so grotesque and terrifying.

One person in a white gown said, "*Yokoni natte!*"

Unable to understand him, both Chunja and Sunhwa stood hesitantly.

"Lie down," interpreted Shiono, who had followed the two of them inside.

Sunhwa lay down on the bed. But the white gown roughly pulled her up. He yelled with annoyance, "*Fukuo nuge!*"

Almost simultaneously, Shiono said, "Take off your clothes and lie down."

Resigned, Sunhwa took off her clothes. As demanded by the white gown, she took off her *jeogori* top as well as her underwear. Her thin figure was thoroughly exposed. Now that she was fully naked, Sunhwa faltered, not knowing where to put her hands. Chunja's face reddened first.

Sunhwa lay her naked body down flat on the bed. As soon as she lay down, the medic in white gown sprayed something on her lower body. White liquid from the spray bottle dispersed throughout the room like a mist. Sunhwa wheezed. The pungent smell of the spray stung her nose like an awl. Chunja coughed as well. The spray left a thin layer of fear like a white curtain over the girls.

"*Yokoni natte* (lie down)!" the white gown yelled at Chunja.

She could guess what the White Gown was saying, but Chunja stood rooted to the spot. From the masculine figure under the gown and the voice, Chunja could tell that the medic was a man.

Once, while bathing in a discreet part of a stream, Chunja had been seen by a man from her village who had come out to get grass for his oxen, and she'd spent the entire day cooped up in the storage shed out of shame.

At a loss as to what to do, Chunja stood with her ears turned red, and Shiono yanked her arm. Chunja staggered. Even before she could steady herself, Shiono pulled Chunja's *jeogori* over her head.

"Why are you so sluggish? Hurry up!"

In an instant, the white skin of Chunja's torso was

exposed. Hugging herself tight with her two arms, Chunja lay down on the bed. A chill went down her spine. Hands in white gloves roughly yanked her arms from around her chest. Chunja's full breasts were exposed. She wriggled and squirmed, struggling to cover them, but the hands lifted her skirt next and pulled down her underwear.

"No!" screamed Chunja.

"They're doing you a favor, giving you a medical exam. So why are you making a fuss!"

Shiono approached her angrily and pressed Chunja's shoulders down with her hands alongside the White Gown.

Like a butterfly pinned to a board, Chunja couldn't budge. An image of a cow hung on the wooden frame at a slaughterhouse flashed before her eyes. She squeezed her eyes shut in shame. But the shame passed in a moment, and a cold piece of metal penetrated her between her legs.

"Ahh!" Chunja screamed at the dull pain.

She tried to get up, but someone was holding her ankles down. The medic sprayed liquid at Chunja too. She coughed a fit from the pungent stench. She wriggled like a caterpillar that had been stomped on by a huge, barbaric foot. Next to her, Sunhwa moaned.

The medic said something to Shiono, who was now wearing a mask. She murmured to Chunja, "You're done. They say you're clean."

Having been freed from the grip of strong hands, Chunja quickly pulled up her underwear that were around her ankles and covered herself with the train of her *jeogori*. She didn't feel any pain. But she shuddered in shame that felt like knives stabbing her from all sides. She couldn't stop wheezing. She was nauseated, and she kept retching. Tears sprang from her eyes as she coughed.

The white curtain at the door fluttered. Through the corner of the door, Chunja could see the eyes of the girls widened in fear.

The medic's irritated voice rang out once more, "*Tsugi no hito!*"

Shiono shouted in a nasty tone: "Next!"

A Party in Hell

Chunja stood awkwardly in the center of the room. She looked around with terror-laden eyes. It was a small room with a high ceiling, like the tobacco drying room she'd often seen around her town. The room wasn't even five or six square meters in size. There was a small window at head height, but it must have been dark outside because no light was coming through. There were fixed bars on the window. It resembled the mouth of a man who'd lost a few teeth. The sudden thought of that window opening its mouth wide and devouring her made Chunja shudder. There was a khaki military mat laid out on the floor. Aside from the mat, there was nothing else in the room, except for a small pouch on top of the mat—the khaki-colored pouch, like the one that Buddhist monks carried to ask for donations, the one that had the words "Advance

First" written on it.

When her thoughts reached the slippery object inside the pouch, Chunja quivered. She plopped down on the mat.

The number of her room was 13. A small wooden tag with the number etched with blank ink hung by the door. On both sides of the door were words written vertically in Japanese: "Dear Japanese soldiers, thank you for your work" and "Please accept my service provided with my body and soul."

Gwang-ok was number 12, and she was in the room to the right of Chunja's. Room number 14 was occupied by the little girl Ok from Hoeryeong. But no sound came from either room. Normally Gwang-ok would've chattered away in a high-pitched voice, but her room was eerily silent.

The girls were miserable after the series of bizarre things they had been subjected to all day. The shameful acts that had been performed on them clung to their skin like bugs with sticky feet.

The medics had touched their breasts without asking permission, made them raise their arms and smelled their armpits. They examined the girls' nostrils to check if they had rhinitis, measured the lengths of their shoulders and waists, inspected their skin color, their belly buttons, and even their toes. The men in white gowns stood with their eyes fixed on the girls' exposed private parts. They freely scanned the girls' bodies with dubious gazes. Those brutal figures seemed as if they were going to lunge at them and rip them apart with the shiny pieces of metal in their hands.

For country girls who several times a day pulled down the cloth of their *jeogori*, afraid that the skin on their backs might be exposed and retied the sashes to keep their budding breasts hidden, what they'd experienced was a ghastly humiliation that made them want to swallow their tongues and die.

When the girls waddled out, halting and stumbling, after the humiliating medical exam, Shiono repeated what she had said earlier. She coaxed, cajoled, and threatened.

"It's all for you girls. If you bear with it a bit and work here, you'll be able to pay back the five hundred won you owe us.

"I don't even know how long you'd have to work at a factory to pay back all that money…

"I'm saying this one more time. This place is miles

away from your towns.

"This is a military camp. You may have come here at will, but it won't be easy to get out!"

With their minds and bodies completely exhausted, the girls didn't have an ounce of energy to respond to her ridiculous statements. They simply took the torrent of words that poured down on them.

Amid the series of terrible misfortunes that came at her in heavy waves, Chunja didn't even have a chance to swim up to the surface to catch her breath. She was afraid that another wave as tall as a house or even a mountain would hit her.

The lightbulb dangling from the ceiling lit up. It wasn't very bright, but the sudden ray of light made Chunja narrow her eyes. Then music came on from somewhere. It began abruptly, like a blindly thrown stone shattering a water jar. Chunja shuddered at the burst of uproarious sound. It was coming from a speaker in the military camp.

The song was full of excitement and passion. The marching song resounded throughout the camp. The sound rushed into Chunja's small room through the small window, like water spurting through the cracks in the dam.

Iron castles on the sea for offense and defense, we trust in you.

Floating castles shall defend the Empire of the Rising Sun to the end.

Iron ships, to the bloody and deadly foe, you strike a heavy blow.

The song was played repeatedly, and the singing that sounded like angry shrieks made Chunja nervous. Against the loud military song, someone was yelling. It was the fat, mean-looking officer Nobuyuki. He was shouting in Japanese, so Chunja didn't understand what he was saying, but just his voice was enough to seize her with fear.

"Begin the operation in two groups, one group of officers and one group of privates. Purchase your tickets first and begin…"

The buzzing of the crowd outside grew louder. Some were cackling.

Nobuyuki's fiery, excited voice rang out again, "Today

the Army Entertainment Center has finally opened!"

"*Kimochi iina* (I'm excited)!" another voice shouted.

The men roared with laughter.

Chunja heard the sound of pounding footsteps, as though a herd of oxen was coming her way. The sound echoed through the hall and rushed at her like a tsunami. She stood perplexed and nervous at the earthshaking rumble, when the door to her room slid open and a soldier clad in khaki uniform stepped inside.

The man rolled his bloodshot eyes to scan Chunja up and down.

"*Kirei* (pretty)!"

With thick black sideburns that resembled bushy pines, the man hurriedly untied the laces on his boots. He held a small piece of paper between his lips. He was so excited that his fingers were all thumbs. After struggling for a while, he finally managed to get his boots off. Then he hurriedly took his shirt off. His chest was hairy. Above all, a wormlike scar across his chest caught Chunja's eyes.

"Goodness!" Chunja exclaimed.

She backed away from the man in alarm. But soon her back hit the wall. As if trying to seep into the wall, Chunja crouched and cowered. Goosebumps covered her skin from head to toe.

The man took the piece of paper from between his lips and waved it in front of her.

"*Miroyo* (look)," he said. "*Nyuujokenda* (it's a ticket)."

He shoved the piece of paper into Chunja's hand. There was a round blue stamp on it. Sideburns grabbed Chunja by the waist and threw her on top of the military blanket. Chunja felt faint as the man's hands raked Chunja's *jeogori* off. The sashes were torn off by his aggression. Desperately, Chunja grasped the plackets of her top to cover her chest, but the man grabbed her skirt this time and tried to pull it off.

"Why are you doing this?" Chunja pleaded piteously. "Don't do this, please!"

She grasped her skirt in her hands. But her flimsy skirt was too fragile to protect her. It was already torn like a dried leaf. The skirt that her aunt had given her, the very first present that Chunja had ever received in her life, was horribly ripped apart.

The man reached out his hands that were as rough and coarse as tree bark and violently grabbed Chunja's breasts. His lips reeking of alcohol scoured Chunja's cheeks and neck. Her budding breasts were squeezed, and the skin on her cheek that had been pressed against the man's beard grew red. The man swooped in on her with all his body. He wrapped his arm around her neck and panted under her earlobes. Heavy as a rock, he pressed down on Chunja.

Stifled under his weight, Chunja struggled. But it was impossible to get out from underneath the man, who was pressing down on her mercilessly with all his weight, as though he were going to make jerky out of her. A blue vein bulged like a snake along Chunja's neck as she struggled.

"Mommy!"

For the first time in her life, Chunja called for her mom to save her.

The door slid open. A woman's round face appeared at the door. It was Shiono.

"Shiono!" Chunja croaked her name. She was begging for even the slightest effort to save her.

But Shiono pretended not to hear her and instead spoke to the man in Japanese, "Make sure to put on 'Advance First.'"

Then she slid the door closed.

Chunja felt despair as if she were sinking into the

water without so much as a straw to grasp at. The next moment, a stabbing pain ravaged her down there, ripping through her despair.

"Help!" Chunja screamed again at the top of her lungs. But no one came to save her.

Overcome with a bestial desire, the man licked, bit, and crushed Chunja like a savage animal tearing into its prey. Trapped firmly between his two tree-like arms and unable to resist, Chunja shook as though she were being rocked in a winnowing basket. Her lower lip must have torn from her biting down on it, because she tasted metal in her mouth. The piece of paper with a blue stamp fluttered down from her hand.

Chunja didn't know how much time had passed, when the rock-like body finally got off her.

Panting, Sideburns pulled up his pants, but even before he finished buckling his belt, another soldier entered the room. The first man cackled as he put on his clothes. Having satisfied his lust, he took his time and sang along with the war song playing outside.

Floating castles shall defend the Empire of the Rising

Sun to the end.

While he tied the laces of his boots, the second soldier impatiently pounced on Chunja. Fatter than Sideburns, he smothered her with his body steeped in alcohol. With his stale breath, he slobbered all over her face. Once again, Chunja felt something penetrate her like a sharp piece of metal. She opened her mouth in pain, but no sound came out. She only stared at the ceiling with her eyes widened.

The lightbulb looked like a glaring devil's eye. The small window with metal bars seemed like a mouth with missing teeth opening up wide to swallow her whole.

"Mom, mommy…"

Groaning through her throat, Chunja thought that she was in a terrible nightmare. If it really were a dream, it was a horrifying one. But the high-pitched military song that was echoing throughout the military camp reminded her that this whole party in hell was real.

The smoke from coals soar into the sky like the dragon of the sea

The echoing roars of guns reverberate like thunder and lightning

Let us ride the waves for miles and miles and bring glory to the empire

The song was loud enough to cover everything, but it couldn't hide the screams that were even louder. Wails, screams, lecherous laughs, harsh obscenities, rough breathing, and cries of pain and grief resounded everywhere. The rooms were partitioned with plywood walls. The thin pieces boards were unable to filter the rampage of noises but instead announced them in brutally vivid detail. Moreover, the military song that shook the speakers was played endlessly on repeat, making the barracks seem to burst with a cacophony of frogs.

In the sea we are corpses submerged in water
In the mountains we are corpses covered in grass

Even in death, we will never leave our emperor's side.

With a shrill scream, Chunja heard someone vehemently kicking the wall from the next room. After a violent wave of battering, part of the plywood wall gave in. Through the gap, a naked girl ran into Chunja's room.

"Chu… Chunja!"

Even under the dim light, Chunja recognized her right away. It was Gwang-ok. Completely naked, Gwang-ok shouted with a face of a frightened child, "I want to go home, Chunja. Chunja!"

Mixed with tears, her scream was as desperate as someone being chased by a wolf in the middle of the night.

"*Chikushou!*" yelled the man who had been lying on top of Chunja as he sat up in surprise.

Gwang-ok and Chunja became tangled up together. Gwang-ok was trembling as though she'd caught a chill. Chunja was also shaking. They embraced each other with their bodies, nearly convulsing as if from electric shocks. Huddled together in a lump, the two of them cowered and squeezed themselves into a corner.

"*Kono yaro* (you stupid bitch)!"

A naked man rushed in from the next room. With his manhood swollen with lust, he seized Gwang-ok's hair. Gwang-ok rolled on the floor. Even as she did so, Gwang-ok reached out her arm and grasped Chunja's hand in hers. Chunja grabbed onto Gwang-ok's hand as well. Like two people trying not to be swept away by a mountainous wave, they held tight onto each other's hand. It felt like they would lose everything if they let go of each other. The two men tried to pull their hands apart. Taking the chance, Gwang-ok bit into one of their hands.

"*Kono buta yaro* (you stupid sow)!"

Screaming like a pig being slaughtered, the man punched her in a flood of madness. When she fell over, he kicked her with both feet. At the flurry of punches, Gwang-ok screamed like someone about to die as she rolled around like a tiny pea. Not knowing what to do to save her, Chunja screamed and screamed.

At that moment, someone else rushed into Chunja's room, panting and puffing. Wearing only her *jeogori* and nothing below, she ran straight into Chunja's arms. Her trembling hand grabbed onto Chunja's wrist like someone hanging from a cliff. Another man's red face appeared at the door to Chunja's room. He was completely naked but for a military cap on his head.

"Save me," the woman begged Chunja. "Please, please save me."

Her voice was hoarse and cracked like a dry reservoir.

The red-faced man said, "What a fucking shit *enkai*

246

(fest), *baka* (stupid bitch)!"

Then he yanked the woman's *jeogori* apart. The garment tore like a piece of paper, and her torso was miserably exposed. There was a red bite mark on her white breasts.

With his short, stubby hands, the man seized the struggling woman's ankles. Then he yanked as if pulling out a couple of radishes from the field. The woman struggled like her life depended on it, but she was no match for the man's brute strength. The hand that had been entwined with Chunja's was helplessly pulled away.

The man left the room, dragging the woman by her ankles as though dragging an animal to a slaughterhouse.

"Help me! Please!" The woman shrieked at the top of her lungs as her hands grasped at thin air.

When Chunja recognized the woman's pale face amidst the chaos, a squeal escaped her lips. The woman who was being dragged out, her body completely exposed and violated, was the organist from the church choir—Yeongsin.

The Fiery Lake of Burning Sulfur

Chunja lay on the mat stretched out straight and rigid like a corpse and stared at the small window. She could see a piece of the sky outside. There were no stars or moon. Only the night sky bearing darkness hung outside the small window, making it look like a piece of grimy cotton cloth with holes.

Chunja was lying completely naked. All the nooks and crannies of her body were exposed under the lightbulb. She no longer felt ashamed. She didn't have the energy to feel ashamed. The women in the adjacent rooms probably looked the same as her.

Every day, the same humiliating acts were performed on her again and again, as if a rusty gear were being forced to turn, despite its groans. like the wheels of a bike with a stretched chain, struggling to spin. The wooden tags were hung in an orderly fashion inside the entrance to the comfort station. There were no names—only numbers.

Chunja was number 13. Since she had arrived at the comfort station, no one had called her name. Instead, she was addressed as "Number 13."

Once, Gwang-ok had called out to her, saying, "Chunja," and Shiono smacked her so hard that her face snapped to the side.

"We are at war here," Shiono said. "You don't have the time to play around, calling each other by your dowdy names. Call each other by your assigned numbers."

At times, some of the wooden tags would be turned face down, which meant that the women with corresponding numbers were either using the bathroom or were suffering from venereal disease.

Chunja didn't know how many frenzied soldiers pressed their bodies against her delicate figure. She didn't want to know. The soldiers swarmed like a colony of fire ants and left after mercilessly crushing the girls' bodies.

It felt like she had somehow fallen into a horrible nightmare and was stuck in it forever, unable to wake up. Through a series of trance-like cycles of pain and suffering, Chunja kept on passing out, coming to, and passing out again. Every joint in her body ached from blood stasis. The sporadic pain that rushed over her was the only thing that made her realize that she was still alive.

By her head was a pile of tickets to the comfort station marked with a blue stamp, and a used "Advance First" was discarded grossly at her feet. When her gaze landed on it, her head throbbed and she felt nauseated.

A group of privates came on a military truck and left, followed by another group of privates who likewise arrived on a military truck. The sound from the truck engine scared the girls, like the roars of a ferocious beast.

Once, more Japanese soldiers came to the comfort station than usual to celebrate their victory in the most recent battle. Even Shiono was summoned to serve the privates.

"But I'm so old now."

When Shiono hesitated, Nobuyuki ruthlessly kicked her in the back.

"Have you forgotten the principle of serving the country while doing your duty for the holy war that the Great Empire of Japan is fighting? Set an example for those Korean girls, and show them what a Japanese woman can do!"

Shiono stood up. She kept on nodding her head like a hen pecking at corn. And without hesitation she took off her clothes in front of the girls, revealing a saggy figure, like a bag that was no longer taut. She chose the first room as hers and went inside.

The entire scene had made Chunja's skin crawl. She couldn't help but be shocked. Her instincts told her that she was held in the grip of the sharp claws of a predatory bird. If there really was a fiery lake of burning sulfur like she read about in the Bible, Chunja thought that this must be it.

While Chunja was "servicing" the soldiers, Shiono had left rice balls and a side dish on the floor by her head. Her empty stomach had long been growling, as though hunger was scratching her intestines, but Chunja didn't have the energy to move at all and left the food uneaten.

Something rustled by her side. Weakly, Chunja opened her eyes. It was a cat. A black cat had entered the comfort station somehow. The cat slowly tiptoed into the room around Chunja and pounced at the food. Its tongue darted in and out, and soon Chunja's rice balls were gone.

The day before, there was a white cat, but today's one was black. For some reason there were quite a lot of cats in the barracks.

The cat with its coarse black coat was close enough for Chunja's fingertips to reach. It lapped at Chunja's water. Thirst coated her tongue, and her whole mouth felt dry, but with no energy to shoo away the cat Chunja only watched its squirming rear end from behind.

On that day, Chunja had counted up to eleven bodies, each as heavy as sacks of salt, that tackled her. After that, she let her consciousness roam free. Torsos drenched in sweat and moist breath mixed with the stench of alcohol, profanities and the experience of being violently violated… Not wanting to see the demon-like faces that were pushed up close to her own, Chunja kept on squeezing her eyes shut, and the only things that she remembered were the damp odor and sound of panting.

It was like she'd fallen into a river, swollen from a heavy downpour on a stormy night. Muddy water poured into her mouth, and she flailed her arms to rise up to the surface, but when she did, another wave of muddy water surged over her. Without even giving her a chance to scream or moan, water rushed up her nose and into her mouth again, as her floundering arms and legs were getting cut and scratched against sharp rocks and broken branches. . . . She felt as though she'd been thrown into this whirling river of hell without even knowing how to swim.

The military song that made her ears bleed all day finally stopped, and soldiers who were wild with overflowing lust no longer entered her room. There were no more screams or sounds of resistance coming from the adjacent rooms.

Even though she'd fiercely resisted, Gwang-ok had been dragged back into her room. And Yeongsin, unexpectedly here in this chaos, had been also hauled back into hers. There were no more sounds coming from their rooms, possibly half-dead from the terrors of the day. There were no sounds coming from any room.

Suddenly there was static from the speaker hung on the rooftop of the barracks, followed by a near shriek.

"*Shoudou* (lights off)!"

Startled out of her wits, Chunja put her hand over her chest. Her heart was beating wildly. Then all the lights in the barracks went out at once.

Once again, a roar came through the speaker, "*Shuushin* (Sleep)!"

As if a huge curtain of silence had fallen, the entire barracks became eerily silent.

Deep in the night, after quivering in unbearable terror for some time, Chunja tried knocking on the plywood wall between her and Gwang-ok's room.

"Gwang-ok, Gwang-ok."

Moments later, a low sound seeped through from the other side of the wall.

"Chunja… how did we…" Gwang-ok was crying.

Neither of them spoke. Instead they cried silent tears for a long time on either side of the plywood wall.

Moments later, Gwang-ok spoke.

"Chunja."

Then after a long pause, she said, "Let's run away."

At her words, Chunja sat bolt upright. Belatedly, she realized that she needed to get away from the humiliation and terror that she'd suffered in full measure. In the darkness, she hurriedly put on her clothes. The moment she stood up, she felt pain between her legs. She slumped, groaning. But she was determined to escape. She crawled out of the room on all fours. Gwang-ok came out of her room as well. In the dark, the two of them groped for each other's hands.

When their warm hands found each other, Chunja felt the tears come. Tightly holding each other's hands, the two of them wandered the corridor, looking for an exit.

A cat screeched in the corridor when the girls passed by. Just then, the light came on in the room at the end of the corridor with a click. A white face appeared. And a sharp voice.

"Who's there?"

It was Shiono. She ran out of the room barefoot and pulled Chunja and Gwang-ok by their shoulders.

"What are you doing? Running away?"

With her hair down and disheveled in the dark, Shiono was the very image of a demon. Chunja lowered her voice and pleaded, "Please let us go, Shiono."

"No!" Shiono yelled. She grabbed Chunja's wrist in one hand and Gwang-ok's in the other.

"Please let us go! Please!" Chunja begged, but the fingers coiled around her wrist like a kudzu root were clenched with a strength that didn't seem to come from a woman.

"I want to go home!" Gwang-ok shrieked and pushed

Shiono in the chest.

Shiono fell on her back. Chunja and Gwang-ok scrambled to run forward. Shiono got up and once again ran over to them, grabbing their shoulders. The three of them fell down together in a tangled mess in the corridor.

At that moment, there was a rushed shuffle of military boots outside. Flashlights danced like flaming swords. The door to the comfort station slid open and a few soldiers promptly rushed in. At the flashlight that blinded her like a knife, Chunja felt faint.

"What? You trying to run away?"

The soldiers grabbed the girls by their collars and hair and hurled them to the floor again. Like eagles snatching away chicks, they dragged the girls away. Gwang-ok and Chunja were hauled back into their rooms.

The bare lightbulb came back on. With the stamping of military boots came the thrashing. Amidst all that was happening, Chunja immediately recognized the harsh, grating and grinding voice that belonged to Nobuyuki.

One of the soldiers smacked Chunja's fear-stricken face with his flashlight. Covering her face, Chunja rolled on the floor.

"*Chikusho*! How dare you try to run away from this

place? This is a military camp, a military camp!"

The man who had hurried over to her room without a shirt on his back and just a military cap on his head hurled insults as he wildly kicked at Chunja's head and torso.

In the adjacent room, Chunja could hear the sound of beating and Gwang-ok's screams.

"Don't hit her face!" Nobuyuki shouted toward the men in Chunja's room.

Chunja didn't remember how that night passed. When she came to, licking her bloodied lips, the small window was brightly lit. She managed to crawl over and knocked on the plywood wall.

"Gwang-ok, Gwang-ok."

She could do nothing other than call for Gwang-ok. She felt that finding Gwang-ok, her blood relative, was the only thing that could help her breathe even for a second in the swelling waves of terror, the only good thing that she could try to grasp for a moment in this vortex of despair.

Gwang-ok made sounds from the adjacent room. Gwang-ok spoke in a lucid voice mixed with tears.

"I'm going to run away. I'm going to escape."

As if she were making a promise to herself, Gwang-ok kept on repeating the words. Listening to Gwang-ok's mutterings, Chunja trembled.

Military barracks enclosed by walls and tight security, soldiers in khaki uniform holding rifles with bayonets standing guard by the gate, the flag of Imperial Japan fluttering in the wind on top of the roof… Chunja recalled the austere and fearsome image she'd noticed on the way in. Squatting on the floor with one hand on the plywood wall between her and Gwang-ok's room, she stopped her tears. Sobs from the adjacent room mingled with Chunja's own.

"Fall in!"

Suddenly a sound rang out from the speaker in the barracks, and Chunja woke from a nightmare.

"Everyone needs to assemble in the yard," Shiono yelled from the corridor. "*Hayaku!*"

Her voice was edged with tension.

The girls who had been weighed down with shame and humiliation in the depths of hell walked out of the comfort station in a group and gathered in the yard, trembling in fear. Covered in yellow dirt, the yard was full of the lingering morning fog and bloody energy. The dense fog seemed to portend a new nightmare to come. The women, their faces pale and thin like a piece of paper from prolonged lack of sunlight, stood in a line across from soldiers standing at attention with rifles on their shoulders, as though they were facing the enemy.

At the front of the line were two German Shepherds on leashes, standing by the soldiers' feet with their tall ears pricked up and their fur standing on end, staring with eyes that seemed to glow an unnatural blue. Their long tongues darted in and out.

With a loud thumping of his military boots, Nobuyuki stepped up to the very front. A cat that had been sitting on a window sill of the comfort station swiftly scurried away.

His imposing presence—the huge, corpulent body, the sides of his head shaved almost white, and the bloodthirsty military uniform—made the girls' skin crawl once more. His face looked even fiercer than before, and the girls stood shuddering like chicks in front of an eagle's open beak, wondering what kind of thunderbolt was about to strike down on them.

"We caught two people trying to escape early in the

morning."

Shiono translated his words into Korean.

"Unfortunately, they were not soldiers but two girls."

At that moment, Chunja felt her heart constrict. She suddenly realized that she hadn't seen Gwang-ok among the girls assembled in the yard. She was frantically looking for Gwang-ok with her eyes, when Nobuyuki's jarring voice rang out again.

"Comforting our soldiers who readily give their lives for the victory of the Great Empire of Japan is a sacred task. Yet two of you attempted to escape, one of whom we caught and the other still tried to run away before being killed."

At his last word, the entire barracks froze as though it had been doused with ice cold water.

The soldiers dragged two bodies in and threw them in front of everyone. One lay completely still, her head face down on the ground, while the other was holding her bloodied leg and rolling on the ground. Exposed under the black skirt, a chunk of flesh on her calf had been torn out, and she was still bleeding profusely. Black blood pooled in a circle within moments in the place she lay rolling. The girl who was groaning, holding her bloodied leg, was Gwang-ok.

"Gwang-ok!" Chunja yelled.

A German shepherd lunged toward Chunja and barked ferociously. It growled, revealing its red gums and sharp teeth. Chunja was rooted to the spot, unable to do anything.

Nobuyuki kicked the body that was lying still on the ground and rolled her face up, saying, "If you try to run away again, this is how you will turn out."

In an instant, Chunja gasped, drawing a sharp breath of surprise. The person who was splayed out in a pool of blood was the tall girl from Gukjaga—Sunhwa.

Shrill screams escaped from the group of girls, and among the loud clamor someone kept on backing away with her eyes widened until she turned around and started running. She sprinted frantically toward the gates. It was Yeongsin.

The woman who had shone brightly with a beauty that was almost blinding was now a flower that had lost its color. She was like a bloom whose petals had been ripped and torn in hail and downpour. Her hair was ratty, and the ties on her *jeogori* had been ripped off such that she couldn't even fasten her top. Her bare white bosom underneath showed through the gaps.

Chunja had no idea how Yeongsin of all people had fallen headfirst into the depths of this hell.

"*Tsukamaero* (get her)!"

Nobuyuki roared, and soldiers stampeded over to her. With a heavy thud, the gates to the barracks closed shut, and a sentry blocked her way. Shrieking at the top of her lungs, Yeongsin scurried about in the camp. Then she made straight for a corner of the base. There was a well there. It wasn't a small one with a thatched roof and a pulley like the ones normally seen in Chunja's and other towns but a big one with a huge opening. And it had long been dry.

Several days earlier, a cat had fallen into the well, but the well was so deep that they couldn't get it out. The cat mewed day and night, and Nobuyuki barked something about it being too loud. Then a soldier rushed over and hurled a grenade into the well. *Boom!* A deafening noise shook the camp, and the unreserved brutality had made the girls shudder.

Yeongsin stopped by the well for a moment and looked toward the sky. Soldiers in khaki uniforms opened their arms and hands like predatory birds spreading their wings and tried to grab her. Like a falling flower petal, Yeongsin threw herself into the well.

A Pipe That Couldn't Be Played

The wooden tag marked "Number 1" was turned face down. It belonged to Shiono. Successive news of the imperial troops' victories rushed in from the front, and soldiers who had finished fighting a battle flooded into the comfort station. As a result, Shiono, who had until now been something of a manager for the girls, also had to service the soldiers like the girls. She'd eventually fallen ill.

The Number 12 wooden tag was taken down. That one was for Ok from Hoeryeong. It wasn't turned face down but taken down. One night, after handling dozens of soldiers, young Ok fainted with her eyes rolled back into her skull. She was bleeding profusely between her legs and in the end had to be taken to the dispensary.

Like a fish gasping for breath, she parted her small lips

and asked pleadingly, "Am I dying? *Unni, unni,* save me. Please help me live."

That night, without even leaving any last words, she died. The young body that had been as sprightly and lively as a fish a few months back when they'd arrived at the military camp was now skinny like a shrike. Her body was too young and fragile to withstand the terrifying and brutal rapes, and after months of struggling to hang onto her precious life with her slender fingertips, she'd let go of it. Her corpse was tossed into the dry well in the corner of the military camp, on top of the corpses of the cat and Yeongsin.

There was no mourning the dead. No one dared to cry. And their tears had already dried up.

Meow! Only a cat sitting on a window sill of the comfort station gave a weak mew, as if to grieve Ok's death.

Yeongsin's wooden tag was also taken down. The wooden tags that had belonged to the deceased were considered bad luck and discarded, and newcomers were given new numbers.

The soldiers had craned their necks like pecking chickens by the well and tried to drag Yeongsin out first, but upon giving up they took out their rifles and shot at her without second thought. And so Yeongsin, who had sung hymns with such a beautiful face, beautiful gestures, and a beautiful voice was trampled so tragically under military boots. Chunja wondered, *Would the deacon who's probably in Gyeongseong (Seoul) now know about all this?*

Gwang-ok, who had been bitten by a German shepherd during her attempted escape, received treatment for only a few days and then had to receive soldiers even before her wounds had begun to heal.

It was at a time like this that even Shiono, the woman who'd once ruled over the girls, had fallen ill.

Even though she'd tussled with the soldiers to put on "Advance First" (military condoms) before service, Shiono had to service dozens of men every day and ended up contracting a venereal disease.

The soldiers were required to use "Advance First" during sexual intercourse. Those who violated this rule and contracted venereal diseases were interrogated and required to submit a written explanation. Yet there were always men who refused to use protection, and the women, tired from having to service dozens of men every day, simply had no energy to even think about condoms each and every time. On these occasions, the diseases never missed their chance to infect the women.

The medics performed STD tests once a week. When one was presumed to have contracted a venereal disease, medics gave them a shot of Number 606. When that didn't work, they sprayed some potent gas between their legs. Later Chunja learned that the gas had been mercury. Shiono received a shot of Number 606 and was sprayed with mercury, but she'd fallen ill in the end.

Chunja was tasked with taking care of Shiono on her sickbed. Chunja didn't even want to see the face of the woman who had been so cruel to her and the other girls, but at least she didn't have to receive the soldiers during the time she had to take care of Shiono, and that felt like a sweet escape from the devil's grasp, at least for a short while.

After being sprayed with mercury, Shiono lay completely naked with just a military blanket covering her. Her body parts that were not covered by the blanket were dry, like wood kindling. The disease had burrowed into her body, growing abscesses here and there, and her lips were blue as though they'd been dyed with something.

Shiono raised her thin forefinger and pointed to a bundle in the corner of the room, asking Chunja to bring it to her. From it, she took out something long that was wrapped in silk. When she unraveled it, something that resembled a pipe appeared. It was a musical instrument that was completely varnished with lacquer, but with a vivid orange hue on the inside that could be seen through the holes.

"This is a *shakuhachi*," said Shiono, her cracked and dry lips moving only so slightly. "They call it that because its size is about one point eight (*hachi*) *shaku* long… it's similar to a Korean *piri*."

Shiono placed the instrument on her stomach. As she fiddled with it, she said, "My husband Sasashiro used to dream of becoming a master *shakuhachi* player."

A smile appeared on Shiono's pallid face.

"Every time he sat dignified, playing the *shakuhachi*, I felt I had the whole world in my hands. He ran a school to teach people to play *shakuhachi* in the Asakusa district in Tokyo. We met through my older brother, who learned to play there, and we got married."

When Shiono randomly began to talk about her past, Chunja looked down at her, confused. Then the vague smile on Shiono's face vanished.

"My husband was drafted for the war and went to fight in Manchuria. And within a few months, my older brother, too…"

Shiono spoke in fluent Korean, and her tone was so serious that Chunja quietly listened to her as she rubbed ointment on the sick woman's abscesses.

"There were thousands, tens of thousands of women who'd sent off their husbands to fight in Manchuria like me. I was worried about whether he was dead or alive, and night and day, I prayed for his safe return, rubbing my hands together until the lines on my palms faded, but I didn't hear anything about him for years. I wrote letter after letter from the agony of missing him, but it was like throwing rocks into a river. Later I found out that most letters sent by soldiers were screened, and they were either confiscated or delivered with most of their contents erased. Around that time came the news of my brother's death. I nearly went crazy. The image of my husband collapsing with blood in his mouth kept on haunting me every night and day. Many women like me urged the Ministry of the Army to allow us to form an organization to find our husbands who had gone to war and visit them in Manchuria. Our demands were rejected, but I couldn't give up. I did everything and anything I could to go to Manchuria, to be near my husband. Then I voluntarily joined the Women's Patriotic Unit and ended up coming here."

Shiono grew quiet all of a sudden.

"What happened next?" Chunja asked.

"Then…" Shiono let out a long sigh. "There were many women like me in Japan then and still now. Many wanted to dedicate themselves to the country by joining not only the Women's Patriotic Unit but also Women's Labor Corps and Special Volunteer Corps. All of Japan was like one huge military camp. Women, as well as students and even the blind, were recruited to work for munitions manufacturers. Women were banned from wearing colorful clothes or getting their hair permed; we couldn't even wear rings. I'd even donated the ring that my husband had given me for the country. We had to give cookware like pots and even children's tricycles as offerings for the war our country was fighting. And rice, candy, matches, and charcoal were all rationed. Despite all of that, we thought that this was the right thing to do for those who were fighting the holy war. We happily accepted it… The first day after I arrived in Manchuria, I was assigned to entertain the officer in charge of the club. I thought all I had to do was to sing and play the *shakuhachi* for the men who'd returned from battle, but I was ordered to give my body to him at night."

Shiono brushed her fingers over the *shakuhachi* once more.

"When I came to Manchuria, I brought my husband's most cherished *shakuhachi* to give to him. I'd learned to play it from him. So I tried to comfort the soldiers with music, but they didn't even glance at the instrument. Seeing me cry, the club's officer rebuked me, saying, 'Comforting the imperial troops with your body is the Women's Patriotic Unit's duty and an act of repaying the country.' I spent every day in tears. Then the officer in charge of the club threw me out, and my situation got even worse. I was sent to somewhere called the Far East Commissariat, and there I had to service infantry soldiers. When they found out that I was Japanese, they all called on me. At some point, I'd even received sixty men in a single day."

Her voice became wet with tears.

"I decided that this was the fate I was dealt and happily

accept it. Servicing dozens of men every day, I shouted 'Come for the Emperor' over and over again to the very last man.'"

Her face contorted with pain. Chunja stopped moving her hands, concerned that she might have touched somewhere that hurt Shiono while cleaning her abscesses. The woman began to speak again. But the pain in her face remained, as though it had been etched on her features. It was the pain from her heart that ran much deeper than any physical pain.

"Most of the girls at that comfort station were Korean. There were some Chinese girls too. I managed them, and I learned to speak Chinese and Korean then..."

She'd been feverish and having a hard time breathing, but today she spoke quietly without a pause, telling a long story and unburdening her heart.

"That day we had a welcoming celebration in the camp for the victorious warriors. Because I could play an instrument, I was selected along with some of the young women from the Japanese Volunteer Corps to get on stage to sing and play music. I was enthusiastically playing the *shakuhachi* when there was a roar from among the soldiers.

"'Stop right now!'

"Everyone had been listening to the music, but the words came like a thunderclap. Then the man who'd roared came up onto the stage all of a sudden and grabbed my wrist. The moment I saw him, my heart almost stopped. It was Sasashiro. My husband, Sasashiro. He dragged me out of the hall. Then he pulled out a pistol and aimed it at my head.

"'You came all the way here, and what have you been doing since then? Why are you dressed like this? And what's with this makeup?'

"He saw that I'd been servicing the soldiers like all the women of the volunteer corps. He pressed the muzzle of the pistol against my forehead, like he was going to shoot me right there. I'd never even dreamed of seeing him at a place like that. He grew angrier, and so I raised my voice too.

"'I came here to offer myself completely for the soldiers of the Great Japan, for the holy war of the Great Empire of Japan, and for the emperor himself, just like you.'

At my words he shuddered and lowered the gun. Then he walked into the barracks. After that he refused to see me. Even when I pleaded with him, saying, 'I came all this way to the battlefield through a hail of bullets to look for you,' and 'I brought the *shakuhachi* that you loved.'

"I went to him every day, and one day he snatched the *shakuhachi* from my arms and threw it on the ground and stomped on it. It broke into two pieces."

Only then did Chunja realize that the *shakuhachi* in Shiono's arms was held together in the middle by threads.

"After that, I never got to see him. Later I heard that he was promoted to lieutenant colonel of his division. A few years after that, I heard the news that he was killed in action at a place called Huabei."

Tears oozed like pine sap from the corners of Shiono's eyes. Drop by drop, tears welled in her eyes that were now hollow like small bowls and soon overflowed uncontrollably, creating paths of tears on her flaky, abscessed face.

Chunja looked down at Shiono. The woman who had been unkind and cruel to the girls, the version of Shiono clad in a beautiful blue *wafuku* and white socks and delightfully clacking her *geta* was no more.

Today, Shiono had completely exposed herself to Chunja without a single shred of cloth to cover herself. It seemed that Shiono was also in hell like the rest of them, and her fate was as tragic as her scarred body.

Several days later, at dusk, Chunja and the other girls were forced to board the truck that had transported them to the comfort station. They were told that the troops were withdrawing due to the circumstances of the war and that their comfort station was also closing.

"*Hayaku, hayaku!*"

The corpulent officer Nobuyuki roared again, and the girls helped each other as they trudged along and climbed up into the high truck as the soldiers holding their rifles yelled at them.

Shiono was carried out on a stretcher. As before, she was wearing her blue *wafuku*. But her beauty was no more. The disease had gotten deep into her bone marrow. Even as she lay on the stretcher, barely conscious, she was still holding a long object tightly in her hands. Only Chunja knew what that was. It was the broken *shakuhachi* held together by threads wound around it.

Meow! Meow! A cat mewed inside the empty comfort station. Upon hearing the cat's cries, Shiono seemed to have regained her consciousness because she struggled to sit up but soon gave up. As she struggled, the *shakuhachi*

275

fell out of her hand.

She stretched her hand out and tried to say something, but no sound came out of her dry throat. The soldier who was following brutally stomped on the *shakuhachi* with his military boots and shattered it to pieces.

Shiono's stretcher wasn't headed to the truck. The soldiers carrying her were heading to a corner of the military camp. Stealing glances at them through the gap between the tarp covering the back of the truck, Chunja felt her chest tighten. The soldiers transporting the stretcher were heading to the well where Yeongsin had jumped in a few months before. They stopped by the well and upended the stretcher into it. The stretcher was now vertical, and Shiono in her blue *wafuku* disappeared into the well.

Before Chunja could stop screaming in surprise, a grenade went off with a boom.

The truck raced through the dark, and the stunned Chunja quivered like a ghost. Someone grabbed her hand tightly. The hand was rough and calloused. The hand's owner whispered quietly into Chunja's ear. It was Gwang-ok. But still in shock from the series of events she'd witnessed, Chunja sat in a daze.

"*Shaberuna* (shut up)!" Soldiers holding rifles who sat in the back of the truck with rifles shouted ferocious warnings.

The truck lurched along the endless narrow path in the mountains. Once again Gwang-ok held Chunja's hand. Gwang-ok's hand was shaking uncontrollably. Chunja's hands were also trembling. This had been happening for a while and she didn't know how to make it stop. The frightful sight that she'd witnessed at dusk was imprinted on her retinas, permanently framing the unforgettable, abrupt scene in her mind.

While Chunja sat in a daze, Gwang-ok whispered breathily into Chunja's ears, "Do whatever it takes to survive, Chunja!"

Then pushing the tarp aside, she jumped off from the speeding truck.

"*Chikusho!*" a soldier shouted in surprise, then quickly rapped on the driver's side of the truck as he yelled something urgently in Japanese.

The truck squealed to a stop. Inertia made the people on the truck fall on their sides. Soldiers jumped off the truck, and Nobuyuki also got out from the passenger's seat.

Gwang-ok, who had rolled on the ground after jumping off the truck, stood up and started limping away hurriedly with the last ounce of her strength. The darkness and the shadow of the forest hid her.

"*Tomare* (stop)!" Nobuyuki yelled like a pig about to be slaughtered. He kept on shouting at the top of his lungs, and at last he pulled out a gun from the holster on his belt and shot at the shadow that seemed to be moving between the trees and grass.

Following suit, other soldiers started shooting at the trees as well. Sparks went off from the muzzles of rifles in the dark. Bullets tore through the forest. The forest shuddered at the gunshots.

"Gwang-ok!"

On the truck, Chunja clutched her chest as she wailed Gwang-ok's name.

Blood Rain

In a windowless room, the rays of light peeking in through the cracks of the door frame created a rectangular silhouette. A rectangular sun went down and a rectangular moon came up. Chunja didn't know how many times that cycle repeated itself.

Working out the spectral rectangular sun and moon in pitch black darkness, Chunja felt the changes of the days and the fact that she was somehow still alive. Her body was dull from fatigue and her mind repeatedly entered and exited the bog of consciousness.

She could hear the rain. In this place, it rained even in the middle of winter. Chunja huddled under a khaki blanket and crouched, making herself small. Cold air seeped in through the wall touching her back, which felt more like a pillar of ice. With the sound of the drizzling rain, Chunja's empty stomach growled, whining in hunger.

The meals provided to the comfort women consisted of watery corn porridge, a dumpling as small as a baby's fist, and pickled bamboo shoots. To the women locked in the punishment room, there was only one meal a day.

The skin on her lower stomach still stung a bit. Chunja slipped her hand under her *jeogori* to touch it. Her fingertips brushed a long bumpy scab, like the path of a worm crawling by. A scar was forming. She shuddered.

She was locked in the punishment room. The room was as tiny as a birdcage; the ceiling was so low that her head touched it when she stood up straight, and the space was so narrow that she had to sit with her knees pulled close to her bosom. The girls who violated the so-called rules at the comfort station were locked up here without exception. They were punished for refusing to service a soldier because they felt ill or for talking back to *okaasan*, who managed the comfort station. Not using "Advance First" was also a reason for being confined.

That day, Chunja had bitten the finger of a military officer who jumped at her in a frenzy. An officer with a red military insignia on his shoulder was very drunk when he entered the comfort station, surrounded by privates. He had a short toothbrush mustache just under his nose, like a small piece of seaweed stuck on the groove between his nose and upper lip.

"*Kirei* (pretty)!"

Toothbrush Mustache staggered over to Chunja and lifted up her chin.

He then fumbled through the pockets on his jacket and pulled out a metal hip flask. He held it out to Chunja.

"*Nomina* (drink)!"

"I don't drink," Chunja said as she turned her head to the side.

She tried to get his jacket off and hang it on the wall. But he grabbed her shoulders and pulled her aggressively toward him. Then he pushed her up against the wall. Clenching her cheeks with his hairy hands, he held her mouth open and poured alcohol into it. The liquid went down the wrong pipe, and Chunja grabbed at her throat and coughed in pain while the man laughed.

On top of that, Toothbrush Mustache refused to put on the "Advance First," and he slapped Chunja, knocking her over when she told him to put it on. Chunja channeled all her energy to endure the humiliation Toothbrush

Mustache was subjecting her to, as he jumped on her like a beast and raped her with almost enough force to crush her.

After he had satisfied his lust, he peeled himself off Chunja. Then staggering, he pulled something off his belt. It was a dagger. The blade gleamed threateningly.

Toothbrush Mustache picked up his hip flask and poured alcohol on the dagger. He licked the drops of alcohol that slid down and fell from the blade. Unsure what the man was playing at, Chunja tracked his movements with a nervous gaze. He took his eyes off the dagger and looked down at the woman, lying exhausted. Then he smiled shadily, his toothbrush mustache squeezed between his nose and lips.

In a flash, he was on top of Chunja again. He sat straddling her. Chunja screamed at the sudden pain that dug into her flesh. Toothbrush Mustache was scratching the pale skin of Chunja's lower stomach with the tip of his dagger.

"Pretty girl, let me leave something for you to remember..."

Toothbrush Mustache was carving his name into Chunja's flesh. Chunja screamed and struggled in pain, but he overpowered her and began to etch his name, character by character on her belly. While he carved his name with one hand, he squashed Chunja's face with the other hand. His middle finger happened to land in her mouth as Chunja screamed. She took the chance and sank her teeth into his finger.

He screamed like a pig being neutered. His already twisted face crumpled like a piece of cardboard.

"*Chosenpi* (Korean bitch)!" he bellowed and punched Chunja in the face.

When Chunja had regained consciousness, she found herself in the punishment room.

About a month or so ago, they'd arrived in Nanjing, away from the deep, penetrating cold. Aboard the horse carriage, Chunja saw a river beside the road. The big and wide river seemed to stretch on for miles. It wasn't frozen even in winter.

"That's the Yangzi River. They say it's the longest in China."

The Japanese woman who greeted the girls at the train station and had them board the carriage spoke in rather awkward Korean. When she saw the girls, she'd raised her cheekbones and smiled, showing a mouthful of snaggle-teeth. As was the custom, the girls called her "*okaasan*."

The carriage entered the gate to the city, and quite a bustling street unfolded in front of the girls' eyes. Buildings soared into the sky; crowds of beautifully dressed people busily moved about; and a strange language reached the girls' ears.

Rickshaws carrying gentlemen and ladies ran past the girls' carriage. *Ding! Ding! Ding!* Sounding a bell, a tram passed them by. The girls watched with fascination and surprise as something that looked like a train car raced through the street.

As Chunja looked around in curiosity at the unfamiliar sight, someone said, "We've come to a city now?"

But even as they rode through that unique scenery, the girls seemed uneasy.

"We're getting farther and farther away from home…" someone mumbled with a sigh.

Hugging her bundle of possessions, Chunja said, "At least it's nice that it's not so cold here."

The building that they were to reside in was a two-story cob house with earthen walls and orange window frames. At the gate hung a signboard that read: "First Army Southern Comfort Station."

There were already other comfort women working there even before Chunja and about thirty other girls arrived. When the carriage carrying Chunja and the girls entered the yard, women in the building looked out through the windows. Their attire was different, and they whispered in a different language. The women whose speech resembled the sound of someone busily hulling sunflower seeds were Chinese.

Someone ran down from the second floor. She stood leaning by the building's entrance and watched Chunja and the other girls alight from the carriage. Chunja glanced at the girl clad in a long *changpao* that covered her from her neck to her ankle bone. She was young with deep dimples on both her cheeks. She stared with eyes full of curiosity at Chunja, who was wearing a white *jeogori* and a long black skirt and sporting a long braid.

Without realizing, Chunja touched the collars of her *jeogori*. The set of new clothes that her aunt had given her when Chunja left had become tattered rags. They were covered in lint and discolored spots. In the front of her top were round spots that might have been blood splatter at some point, and they were impossible to get out no matter how many times Chunja had tried to wash them off.

When Chunja's eyes met the girl's, the girl averted her gaze. Her black eyes twinkled with curiosity, but after a moment they were drawn to the ground, losing their sparkle. When Chunja looked again, they were lifeless. They were helpless, like the empty abyss of a dried-up well, desperately yearning to be saved. From the girl's eyes, Chunja recalled another set of eyes: those of Hyesuk, the girl from Yongdeurechon.

After Gwang-ok had jumped off the speeding military truck, causing a disruption, the truck was on its way again. As Chunja wept, the truck raced on and on through the mountains and dropped the girls off at some temporary train station, where they boarded a train once again. Chunja hated trains that seemed like wriggling pythons. The first time she'd carelessly gotten on a train in curiosity, but it had run through tunnel after tunnel and deposited her in hell.

This time around, they were on a freight train instead

of a passenger type. The soldiers had slid open the huge iron door and pushed the girls inside as if loading goods. Only layers of straw covered the cold floor. The car was pitch black inside, making it impossible to see anything. The girls were barely able to tell each other apart by the elbows and shoulders that touched as well as the nervous breath that escaped their mouths.

The train rattled in rhythm with Chunja's heartbeat.

"Where are they taking us now?" Chunja asked out of fear as she brushed the floor with her hands like the blind in the dark. Someone took her restless and scared hands in hers.

"Hyesuk? Is that you?" Chunja asked, recognizing her hands.

Hyesuk only breathed a long sigh instead of answering her.

No one knew how late in the night it was. Only the sound of the train echoed obstinately in their ears.

From every stormy wind that blows, from every swelling tide of woes

Out of the blue, Chunja began to sing. She felt like she

had to do something to shake off the fear that bound her tightly in this darkness.

There is a calm, a sure retreat; 'Tis found beneath the mercy seat.

She sang the hymn "From Every Stormy Wind That Blows." It was the song that Jang Mo-se had taught the people at the church in Deer Valley way back when.

Chunja thought to herself, *The teacher with the smooth, broad forehead dressed in a brown suit. Where is he now? Does he know of the stormy winds and tide of woes that we are experiencing? Does he know that his beloved Yeongsin was raped by savage brutes and fell into the depths of hell? And how is Gwang-ok now? Was she shot dead or did she survive, left to wander the forest? Does the teacher know of the ordeals and difficulties that we are facing? Does the Lord know?*

When she thought of Gwang-ok, Chunja clutched her chest, feeling the pain of her heart being ripped out. The tears she thought she couldn't produce because she'd cried all the tears she had in this life began to flood down her face again, like water pouring from a burst dam.

There is a scene where spirits blend, where friend holds
fellowship with friend;

Chunja sang the hymn to the very end, her voice
choked with tears. Hyesuk sat by her side and hugged
her shoulders close. She took Chunja's hands in hers
and pulled them close to her chest. Just like Chunja's,
Hyesuk's chest rose and fell to the rattling of the train,
running on the rails of sorrow.

With a loud clatter, the train stopped at a station. The
huge iron door slid open. The cold rushed into the train
car with bright light, and the girls squinted. The bright
light was coming from flashlights. Dozens of flashlights
sliced the girls' bodies in the dark like a rampage of
swords. A horrible shriek of laughter burst out from the
crowd outside. Behind the flashlights, Chunja made out
the red insides of the gaping mouths of the laughing
soldiers.

Nobuyuki walked out and faced the men with a paper
megaphone in his hand. He clicked his heels together and
bowed, bending his torso forward so that it was nearly

parallel to the ground.

"Soldiers of the Imperial Army who have been fighting the holy war, thank you for your hard work! Please receive the service we provide with our hearts and bodies. You have only one hour, so get into three groups, one for each car. For your own health, make sure to use 'Advance First.'"

A few of the soldiers cackled as they passed out condoms from the military sacks that Nobuyuki handed them.

"For your own safety, make sure to use 'Advance...'" Nobuyuki repeated into the megaphone, but even before he finished his sentence, the soldiers pushed him aside and jumped up onto the train cars.

"*Goyukkuri tanoshinde kudasai* (take your time and have fun)!"

Nobuyuki shouted at the top of his lungs, veins bulging from his neck, but the frenzied soldiers were like a flood bursting a dam. The soldiers pushed through, and Nobuyuki spun around like the blades of a pinwheel, the megaphone dropped from his hand and rolled on the ground.

It was the image of a pack of wolves racing down from

the mountains to attack a poultry farm full of young chicks. The soldiers pushed each other as they climbed up onto the train cars and knocked down the comfort women. The train cars were filled with appalling screams and horrible laughter. The soldiers who didn't make it onto the train cars in time shone their flashlights inside and cackled.

"Get it over with quickly!"

"Stop dawdling!"

"I'm up next!"

Impatiently, some even screamed obscenities at the top of their lungs.

Right then, a song erupted from the station building. Chunja shuddered at the belligerent burst. It was a tune she knew very well. It had resounded throughout the yard of the military camp and completely shook up all the women there on that day, the day she was brought to the camp from some unknown station and lost her virginity. The marching song came from the speaker hanging on the rooftop of the station building and echoed throughout it.

Iron castles on the sea for the offense and defense, we

trust in you.

Floating castles shall defend the Empire of the Rising Sun to the end.

Chunja and Hyesuk lay spreadeagled on the floor of the train car, their heads touching. As the pack of wolves climbed on top of them and unleashed their lust, the girls' heads bumped against each other. Their eyes met. The eyes that Chunja saw through flashes of light in the darkness were helpless and hopeless. She had never seen such pitiful eyes before. Chunja closed hers.

Floating castles shall defend the Empire of the Rising Sun to the end.

The quivering flashlights and the loud song that pounded the listeners' ears buffeted, shook, and pummeled the girls' bodies.

After some time, the savage fiesta was over. But even before the girls could pull themselves together, Nobuyuki jumped onto the train and said, "Numbers 17, 21, 23, 36, and 42. Come out."

He shined the flashlight on the girls' faces one by one

and called on about ten of them. The girls whose numbers were called got off the train as Nobuyuki roared at them. They staggered off. Hyesuk was among them. Because of the pain between her legs, she couldn't stand, instead squatting down on the ground with her arms wrapped around her stomach.

To one corner of the station yard, a truck raced in, flashing its headlights like huge eyes. It stopped immediately in front of the girls. As Chunja watched the scene unfolding before her eyes, an uneasy feeling began to fill her heart.

"*Nore, nore* (get on, get on)!" Nobuyuki shouted, pushing the girls on the ground. "Due to the demand from the troops, you will be transported elsewhere."

As she was about to get on the truck, Hyesuk looked toward Chunja. Once more Chunja saw her helpless and hopeless eyes. Hyesuk stood frozen to the spot, her eyes glued in Chunja's direction and tears streaming down her face.

Chunja, who had been lying on the floor of the train car, pushed herself up onto her elbows. Then she called to Hyesuk with her hoarse voice, "Hyesuk!"

At that moment, the iron door slid and slammed shut

with a screech. The screeching sound of the iron door cut Chunja's voice short. With a roar like that of a beast, the train whistle blew. The train lurched back for a moment and began to move forward.

Usually the girls were locked in the punishment room for only a day. The punishment for breaking important rules only lasted two or three days and no more. But Chunja's time there was much longer. She'd been locked up here before. It was after she was caught trying to escape.

When she thought of Gwang-ok jumping off the truck all by herself, Chunja didn't want to stay in this unfamiliar place for even a second. She regretted not having mustered up her courage to run away too. But when she had managed to escape from the comfort station, she hesitated, disoriented in front of the roads that stretched in different directions. Her pursuers immediately caught up to her and dragged her back to the comfort station by her hair. After being beaten until her eyes were swollen, she had been locked up in the punishment room for two days.

Chunja thought that perhaps she was being punished

for longer this time around because of her previous record. From the scabs that had formed on her stomach, she assumed that she'd been stuck in the room for over a week. She recalled the words that Toothbrush Mustache had spat at her.

"Chosen omago."

It was a derogatory term for Korean comfort women like Chunja.

Chunja had grown up listening to her mom swear and curse until her ears bled. But those were only words that her mom spat out as a habit in the endless throes of life, words she spoke out of love for her precious child.

But the insults that the Japanese men hurled at her were different. They often spat out obscenities between their teeth with a look of contempt, battering the girls' pride and self-esteem senseless and completely wearing them down to the point they were irrecoverable. Those insults dug into the girls' flesh, crushed their bones, and stuck in the depths of their marrow.

"Chosen omago" were precisely the words that Nobuyuki had hurled at the girls all the time. Chunja had been glad that she didn't have to see his fat face anymore, but she had to hear the same words again like a whip that

lashed at her.

Locked up in the punishment room, she had been happy at first because she didn't have to see those ghoulish faces of the Japanese soldiers. But as time wore on in the tiny room full of cold and intense darkness, she'd grown apprehensive. They'd stopped bringing her a dumpling and porridge, which had been given once a day. She thought perhaps they'd decided to starve her to death. But above all, she was thirsty. She tasted a bit of blood from her lips, rough with cracks and scabs from chewing on them.

Trying to figure out what was happening outside, Chunja pressed her ear to the locked door.

The punishment room was in an abandoned house located on the other side of the wall that encircled the two-story comfort station. When the wind blew in the right direction, she could hear the sounds from its second floor. On some nights, she even heard singing. They were songs the Chinese comfort women sang.

The young comfort woman with deep dimples in her cheeks called Xiao Tang often played an instrument and sang. The instrument that she played was called a pipa, and it had four strings on something that looked like a tortoiseshell. Xiao Tang grew out the fingernails on her right hand, perhaps to play better. When she plucked the strings with those fingernails, a pure melody came out of it. With a silky thin voice that matched the clear sound of the pipa, she used to sing.

The castle of Jinling is big and tall
Eighteen ri *inside, eighteen* ri *outside*
Its scenery is known to be the best in the world.

The melody was beautiful, but on bleak nights with a winter breeze it sounded miserable and pitiful.

They didn't understand the Chinese lyrics, but Chunja and the Korean girls also shed tears listening to the song.

On days the soldiers came, the girl with a silky thin singing voice cried out in high-pitched screams.

"*Itai* (It hurts)! *Itai!*"

Trying to communicate the physical pain she felt to the beastly men, she yelled the only Japanese word that she'd learned. But the brutes who lost all their senses to lust never lent an ear to her cries. Sometimes they even locked her in the punishment room for making a fuss of nothing.

Once, Xiao Tang flung her pipa onto the ground while

singing. Then she began to weep loudly.

Because of the language barrier, the Korean girls and Chinese girls only communicated with their eyes. But at that moment, Chunja could guess the meaning of her tears. She understood.

The next day, Xiao Tang rewound the broken strings on her pipa. She tied red tassels to the conical pegs. Then she held up the instrument for Chunja to see. A smile appeared for a moment on her wan face. With the newly decorated pipa in her arms, Xiao Tang began to sing again.

The castle of Jinling is big and tall
Eighteen ri *inside, eighteen* ri *outside*

But now there was no singing that Chunja could hear. The place where Chunja and the Korean girls arrived had been chaotic from day one.

Boom! Boom! Even in the punishment room, Chunja could hear the roars from cannons every now and then. There were loud pops from rifles as well. The pops that resembled the sound of roasting peas continued night and day. Sometimes she could hear the sound of wheels grating across the ground like the growling of a huge beast.

She could also hear the snaggle-toothed *okaasan* yelling at the girls.

"Don't go anywhere!"

"We are at war. You must not take one step outside the comfort station. Never!"

Then at some point everything went quiet. The silence increased her unease.

"Anyone out there?" she called. "Is there anyone out there?"

No one answered her.

"*Darega kite* (anyone there)?" she even shouted in the Japanese she'd learned during her time at comfort stations.

But the outside was as quiet as being underwater.

Chunja banged on the locked door. Then she started kicking at it. The rubber shoes she'd worn on top of her frayed *beoseon* socks were in tatters, the soles much too soft. Her feet hurt from kicking at the door, but Chunja kept at it out of desperation. Like someone trying to swim to the surface of water, she gave a strong kick with a scream. The wooden door broke apart. A sudden gush of cold air rushed in. Her whole body shuddered in the cold. She quickly pulled the khaki blanket around her head and shoulders. Then she staggered out of the punishment room.

Having been locked up in the dark room, the bright light outside made her faint, and Chunja shielded her eyes with her hands.

The comfort station was empty. She didn't know when the army withdrew, but the entire compound had been cleaned out. There was no one—not the dozens of Korean girls who had been brought here on a train, not the haughty and arrogant *okaasan* who spoke awkward Korean and Chinese, not the baby-faced Xiao Tang. Even the signboard for the comfort station that had hung by the gate was gone.

With the blanket wrapped around her, Chunja stepped out into the streets. Afraid that someone might come chasing her, she glanced back at the comfort station. But no one came after her. As she hurried her steps, something caught her eyes. The moment she recognized what it was, a wave of fear surged through her.

It was a pipa. It was the pipa that Xiao Tang used to play. There were red tassels hanging from the pegs, so it was most definitely Xiao Tang's. Its pear-shaped body was cracked and broken, and the snapped strings fluttered in the air like dead octopus tentacles. Dirtied red tassels flailed in the bleak wind.

Xiao Tang had cherished the instrument. Once when Chunja stared at it in curiosity, she'd let Chunja hold it. Chunja had carefully plucked the strings of the instrument that made sounds like the strings of a *gayageum*.

Ting! A clear and crisp sound resonated. The two looked at each other and let out an awkward, plaintive laugh.

The broken pipa reminded her of Xiao Tang's white face, and apprehension rushed into her. Chunja had no idea what happened, and her imagination of the unknown doubled her fear like noodles in soup swelling up over time. She glanced once more toward the comfort station. When she saw the orange gates and window frames, Chunja felt a rush of fear again. Unable to control her imagination and terror, Chunja began to run.

Her starved body was like that of a scarecrow in the winter wind. But flailing her arms and legs, she began to run with all her might. She ran, only thinking that she needed to get far away from the comfort station. When she ran out to the street, an inland port spread out before her eyes.

Then in the next moment, Chunja stood frozen to the spot. Like someone still stuck in a nightmare, she opened her eyes wide to see if the sight in front of her was real. What was it that she'd seen at the port by the rolling river?

There were piles of something. They looked as tall as mountains. At first, Chunja thought they were goods that needed to be loaded onto ships. But when she looked at them again, she felt blood rush to her head.

They were…

They were corpses.

They were piles of corpses.

Corpses were piled up as high as houses and mountains. Like pieces of tattered clothes, they lay twisted, and the bloodied faces were crumpled in grotesque expressions. Blood had pooled near the piles, and it had clotted, turning the ground orange.

Dozens of coolies wearing gloves were cleaning up the corpses from the port. They picked them up and threw them into the river from the top of the breakwater.

Wearing indifferent faces as if they were transporting bricks at some construction site, the coolies hoisted the bodies together and threw them into the Yangtze.

The dead bodies were piling up on the river bed, forming a new dam. The men's gloves were red from blood. Every time they dropped a corpse into the river, the unfrozen water of the Yangtze River below the breakwater splashed upward. The splashing water and foam were tinted scarlet. The reddish waves licked the breakwater like the tongue of some water demon.

Suddenly nauseated, Chunja squatted down and retched. She vomited acid squeezed up from her empty stomach. Then she stepped on something soft. Startled, Chunja jumped to the side. The thing that she'd stepped on was an arm. A severed arm. She staggered and sidled in shock, when her feet ran into something again. It was a corpse. Pieces of corpses were being trodden under her aimless feet.

Chunja shrieked and shrieked. But people passing her by on the street didn't even glance her way. The city swept by a torrent of blood was steeped in eerily silent resignation. Carrying bundles and luggage in their arms and on their backs, people with faces as white as sheets and full of resignation hopped over the corpses in the streets as they hurried somewhere. Severed heads rolled at times like balls, caught in the tracks left by people's footprints. Their busy steps reflected their desperation to get out of this city of hell as soon as possible.

Chunja looked around and noticed that the entire downtown was in ruins, as though someone had poured filth and trash all over it. Everything she laid her eyes on was broken. The buildings, city walls, trees, vehicles, and even people…

Corpses were strewn about here and there throughout the four streets surrounding the port. Houses had been burned down, the city walls had fallen, and there were more corpses piled up along the edges of the walls.

Somewhere, a woman wailed as if she were vomiting up blood. The wailing would have made this horrendous scene more real, but her cries stopped within moments. It seemed that the people of this city had forgotten how to cry anymore.

Trucks were coming to the port, and all of them were carrying corpses. When one truck dumped out all the bodies like cargo, the next one came and deposited yet more bodies.

This is a dream, Chunja thought. *This must be a terrible nightmare.*

In this abysmal, nightmarish pit, Chunja convulsed as if she were trying to wake from sleep paralysis.

Rain began to fall. The drizzling winter rain brought with it the smell of blood. The rain dissolved the clotted blood on the ground, letting it flow in streams.

In the rain and the wind, Chunja's black skirt rustled and fluttered. In the bloody winter rain that blurred the boundary between the sky and the land, she stood rooted to the spot in a devastated daze.

Part III

Haruko's Nanjing

Haruko had never even dreamed of traveling to Nanjing on her first trip to China. She'd boarded the plane with an excitement she couldn't hide at the thought of visiting her boyfriend's hometown and meeting his parents. But having arrived at his small hometown populated by ethnic Koreans, Haruko was in a panic, to the point she could barely pull herself together.

Perhaps this was what it felt like to watch an endless performance of musical theatre with a narrative that stirred up a maelstrom of emotions without even giving you time to catch a breath. In the past few days, Haruko's entire world had turned upside down.

The story that Jonghyeok's grandmother—the woman whose name was written with the same Chinese characters as hers—coughed up slowly over the course of two days was pure horror for Haruko. She couldn't stop her screams at times, as if she were watching a horror film. She was shocked that her own country, Japan, was the villain of such a terrifying story.

To Haruko's generation, the issue of comfort women was only a dramatized story, like an uninteresting scene in some period drama that was too brief to even warrant attention. Many even doubted whether something so dreadful had actually happened. Only when she started dating a Korean man did she start watching the news and television programs on comfort women, as it was a knot that the two of them would have to unravel at some point.

It had just been a story to Haruko, like some vague silhouette of a play that she'd seen from the back row. But her boyfriend's grandmother had been a comfort woman!

She'd easily read the turbulence of emotions in Jonghyeok's heart. He wore a hardened expression on his face the entire time. Haruko had never seen him look so grim; his face had always gleamed with a gentle smile.

Leaving Haruko aside despite having brought her all the way to his hometown, Jonghyeok spent time with the people who were part of the Coalition for Comfort Women Issues. His face was ashen as he listened to the coalition's recording of Grandma's story. After that, he'd been lost for words.

A few days later, Jonghyeok had paid for him and Haruko to follow the Coalition for Comfort Women Issues all the way to Nanjing. He'd voluntarily become a member of the coalition. Jonghyeok wanted to find out more about the truth of Grandma's story. While listening to the last part of her account on the small tape recorder, Jonghyeok had shrieked in a hoarse voice.

"My grandmother went all the way to Nanjing, where that accursed massacre took place?"

His face was crumpled like a piece of paper.

The Coalition for Comfort Women Issues was scheduled to investigate the current conditions of surviving comfort women in northeastern China and then to head to Nanjing, following the tracks of Korean comfort women. Jonghyeok readily decided to join them.

"Let's do it, Haruko," said Jonghyeok. "Let's go to Nanjing."

It wasn't easy to find plane tickets at such short notice. The members of the coalition had already booked theirs online before they arrived in China. Jonghyeok decided to travel by train and meet them in Nanjing. Without even asking for Haruko's input, he booked two rail tickets.

Haruko hesitated but ended up boarding the train, led by her boyfriend. She wanted to travel to Mount Baekdu, about which she'd heard more than enough from Jonghyeok, and she wanted to visit Myeongdongchon, the birthplace of the Korean "poet of the stars" who had died in Fukuoka. She wanted to taste the lamb skewers and cold noodles that were to die for. She wanted to spend time with her boyfriend and enjoy the scenery and flavors of a foreign country. But her boyfriend was in no such state of mind.

The train raced along the tracks for an entire day and night. Riding on a cross-country train for the first time, Haruko felt herself submerged in something like the pleasure of traveling. But even on the train, Jonghyeok was still feeling down. The attentive boyfriend who had talked to her and explained various things to her in a sweet voice was no more. With an indifferent face that resembled a paper mask, he sat quietly. His eyes were red from not having gotten enough sleep in the past few days.

Jonghyeok had bought a bottle of liquor from a convenience store at the train station. It was Kaoliang liquor, 38 percent alcohol by volume. He calmly drank this liquor, which was much, much stronger than the Taru Sake made of rice and chrysanthemums that Japanese people like to drink. Then he drank *soju*, while snacking on tea eggs, which he'd also bought from the convenience store. He'd said that he didn't hold his liquor well, but he'd downed half a liter of strong drink straight out of the bottle.

After an entire day and night, the train arrived at Nanjing Station the next morning. It was the first time that Haruko had spent such a long time on a train, and she was so tired that she lay nearly collapsed on her bed. She got up every now and then to check on Jonghyeok, but he sat still by the aisle, looking at the passing scenery outside. The faint guard lights in the aisle made his silhouette seem like a paper cutout glued to the window.

While packing up his backpack among the other passengers busily moving about, Jonghyeok finally noticed Haruko looking glum and said, "Let's first take a look around Nanjing, and since Shanghai's not far from there we should stop by Pudong for a few days before we head back."

The forty-something team leader of the Coalition for Comfort Women Issues, who had arrived the day before, came with a Chinese interpreter to the station to greet Jonghyeok and Haruko.

"They're family of a comfort woman," the team leader introduced Jonghyeok and Haruko to the translator. Haruko winced. Without even noticing it, she'd become family of a comfort woman.

"*Nin hao* (hello)."

With a grave face, Jonghyeok bowed his head toward the interpreter. Then he talked to her for a few moments in Chinese.

Their guide was a professor surnamed Zhang from Nanjing University, who was the first to research the comfort women issue in China.

"Let's go to Qinhuai District," Professor Zhang told the driver.

Befitting its role as the capital of Jiangsu Province, Nanjing boasted the prestige of a city and the stately features of mainland China. In the streets crowded with people and vehicles, the van carrying the coalition together with Jonghyeok and Haruko was gridlocked by traffic. But Haruko was happy because she could survey the streets, which were a balanced composition of historical sites and modern buildings.

Jonghyeok sat, his face glued to the window of the van, watching everything outside as if he were scanning the streets and alleys of Nanjing. It seems like he was trying to take in the true image of the desolate city that his grandmother had wandered with hesitant steps and a hollow heart.

"There are many army brothel buildings that have survived on Liji Lane (利济巷) in Qinhuai District," explained Professor Zhang. Sporting an elegant bob, she spoke in a voice that was an octave above everyone else's, plainly displaying her excitement.

"Even a few days ago, I attended a meeting at the National Cultural Heritage Administration and insisted on the value of conserving the comfort station buildings. Our research has confirmed over forty comfort stations in Nanjing to date."

"Forty?" the people in the van asked in surprise.

"These are important cultural institutions that can attest to Japan's brutality," explained the team leader. "We cannot let them disappear in the whirlwind of development. They should never be torn down or relocated. We need to preserve them in their original state, like the Auschwitz concentration camp, to show the historical truth."

"That's right," Professor Zhang spoke animatedly with a strong accent. "We asserted that the area should be designated as a 'Major Historical and Cultural Site Protected at the National Level' and preserved in its original state. The protection of a cultural site can clash at times with commercial development, so the government needs to take steps to resolve the conflict. Not only should we preserve the comfort station buildings, but I also believe that we should build a museum to commemorate and pay our respects to the comfort women."

Jonghyeok translated her words to the members of the coalition before the interpreter could. Even the Chinese interpreter quailed at his fluent Chinese and Korean. She did a fine job of interpreting, but occasionally she glanced over at Jonghyeok for confirmation.

Jonghyeok's face was flushed. He was desperate, as if seized by something.

Professor Zhang continued, "As you know, the 'comfort women' system was an important national policy of the Japanese militarist government. In the winter of 1937, the Japanese military invaded Nanjing, and comfort stations began to be established here at the order of

315

Iwane Matsui, the commander of the Central China Area Army. He caused the bloodbath in Nanjing, and after the Potsdam Conference he was indicted for his role in the Nanjing Massacre and executed at the International Military Tribunal for the Far East.

"From the summer of 1937, the Japanese began an indiscriminate bombing of Nanjing. There's a thriving shopping street near Huai Qingqiao, where Mr. Kim Gu resided at the time."

"Ah!" the coalition members exclaimed in unison.

"People say that the roof of his residence collapsed from the bombing. About a hundred key figures of the provisional Korean government and their families had fled Nanjing three weeks before the massacre and gone to Changsha. Had they been a little later, the provisional government might have ended here."

With an extensive knowledge of Chinese and Korean history, Professor Zhang continued to explain, "At the Jilin Provincial Archives, there are 100,000 reports and documents that had been kept by the Japanese Far East Army. Even just recently, researchers found a number of records on Korean comfort women. According to them, there were thirty-six Korean comfort women in Nanjing at the time of the Nanjing Massacre."

After inhaling and exhaling a long breath, Professor Zhang said, "There is also a record of one Korean comfort woman servicing 267 Japanese soldiers over the course of ten days."

A heavy silence fell inside the van.

Honk! Honk! The driver, who was barely driving on the road that was jam-packed with vehicles, blared the horn irritably.

Jonghyeok frowned at the harsh sound, but Haruko wished that he would keep on honking. She couldn't stand the heavy silence that filled the car. Sitting all the way in the back of the van, she pretended to look at her phone the entire time. Haruko didn't even open her mouth, afraid that someone might notice that she was Japanese. The members of the Coalition for Comfort Women Issues hadn't noticed that she was Japanese in the past few days she'd spent with them. When she had to say something, Haruko spoke cautiously in Korean, and they seemed to assume that the hesitant way she spoke Korean was just the way ethnic Koreans from northeastern China spoke. They seemed to regard her as a timid, reserved girl, as she sat quietly with a smile on her lips.

The van finally came to a full stop in an alley. The address was Lijixiang number 18. A decrepit two-story building had managed to remain standing, surrounded on all sides by modern structures. It was a building with old roof tiles, blue walls, and orange window frames.

"You know that picture? The most well-known one among all the comfort women photos taken by the Allied Forces in 1944, featuring a pregnant Ms. Park Young-shim? She was here in this very place."

Professor Zhang withdrew a large copy of a photograph from an envelope. Haruko stole a glance at the picture in her hand. Comfort women were standing or squatting with desultory looks on their faces next to a soldier armed with a rifle. Among them, a woman who seemed to be in the last months of pregnancy stood leaning against a pile of dirt with one hand on her stomach.

Led by Professor Zhang, the coalition members walked around the comfort station building, taking notes and photographs. Professor Zhang explained, "This house used to be a rice store owned by the father of a *dada* (meaning "uncle," any middle-aged man) surnamed Man, but it was confiscated by the Japanese military and turned into a comfort station for the Japanese soldiers. A Japanese trading company was established nearby as well. According to Man *dada*, they called this place Japanese *yaoyao* (窑窑) at the time. In Chinese, *yao* (窑) means coal pit or cave, but it also means house of prostitutes. Man *dada* passed away a few years ago, but he gave a testimony of his vivid memories from that time, when he was about ten years old. After the Japanese withdrew, he got the house back, and he said he found a lot of rubber pouches inside. They were in small boxes made out of kraft paper. And the rubber pouches were printed with the words 'Advance First'…"

The interpreter and Jonghyeok took turns translating Professor Zhang's words to the coalition. The words "Advance First" had been firmly etched in Haruko's heart these past few days.

"There were also tubes of ointment with the words *xingbigao* (星秘膏). The ointment was for preventing STDs. The tubes are currently on display at the museum, and it says on the containers that they were manufactured and produced at the 'Army Sanitation Material Factory' or the 'Army Supply Factory.' There are specific directions for using the ointment as well. Man *dada*'s family opened the rice store again afterward, but people no longer called it the rice store. Instead, they called it *yaoyao*. The comfort stations where Korean comfort women stayed were called '*Gaoli yaoyao*,' meaning 'Korean *yaoyao*.'"

No one spoke. Haruko carefully touched the window frame of the building where the lacquer finish had come off as if it were a fragile structure that would collapse at even the slightest touch.

"*Yaoyao*," she quietly mumbled the word in her mouth. She couldn't imagine the shame and the pain that was contained in that simple word.

Professor Zhang continued, "Unfortunately, Nanjing became the city with the largest number of comfort stations and comfort women established in the eight years that Japan waged war against China. In 2014, some of the old sites of comfort stations were designated as 'Major Historical and Cultural Sites Protected at the Municipal Level' by the Nanjing city government. They mainly housed Chinese and Japanese comfort women, and Korean comfort women mostly stayed in the alley known as Chengxi Tieguan Alley. It was located on today's Sihuan Road, and the comfort station was called the 'First Army Southern Comfort Station.' There was another one by Xishan Road, called the 'First Army Northern Comfort Station.'"

Professor Zhang then looked around at the coalition members and asked, "Have any of you read *Dream of the Red Chamber*?"

It was an unexpected question.

"You know, *Dream of the Red Chamber*, one of China's Four Great Classical Novels," she repeated.

Everyone stared at Professor Zhang with curious expressions.

"Originally Liji Lane and its vicinity were famous as the birthplace of Cao Xueqin, author of *Dream of the Red Chamber*. But it became known to the world more recently with the discovery of Japanese comfort stations."

Professor Zhang breathed a sigh.

The coalition took a group photograph in front of the comfort station building. Haruko volunteered to take the picture. She felt she didn't belong in the photo. Haruko carefully felt for the shutter as if she were touching an old scar and pressed it until she heard it click.

The members of the coalition who had come to Nanjing looking for traces of comfort women busily explored its streets like spinning tops. Jonghyeok, who'd joined them voluntarily, also devoted his sweat and efforts on the streets as a translator. Their last stop was the Nanjing Massacre Memorial Hall.

Haruko had followed Jonghyeok along on this trip, but she became hesitant at the exit of the subway station on Line 2 of Nanjing Metro.

At the exit was a huge road sign that directed people to the Nanjing Massacre Memorial Hall. Its official name was the "Memorial Hall of the Victims in the Slaughter of Nanjing by Japanese Invaders."

It was frightening to see the Chinese characters for "slaughter," usually used to refer to the killing of animals. In Japanese, the word is translated as "*gyakusatsu* (虐殺)," which meant "massacre," like the English translation.

Starting with that one, there were road signs denoting the museum every few hundred steps. Their impact was quite overwhelming.

When she arrived at the memorial hall, Haruko stopped. A huge sculpture as tall as a building was blocking her way. A mother clad in tattered clothes was staring into the sky and wailing, and in her hands was not some object but the limp corpse of her baby.

Haruko shuddered at the violent image of the sculpture that seemed to embody all the words that could express despair—tragedy, grief, mourning, and more. She looked at Jonghyeok with a face full of reluctance. She shook her head from side to side, signaling that she didn't want to go inside. Her gaze was more of a plea.

Without a word, Jonghyeok nodded at her. He realized, a bit belatedly, that it couldn't be easy for a Japanese person to enter the memorial hall. Jonghyeok told Haruko to wait at a coffee shop nearby. They decided to meet at the main entrance of the memorial hall an hour and a half later. Everyone except Haruko entered the hall. She left quickly as if fleeing the scene.

As she entered an alley with hurried steps, an antique market was unrolled in front of her eyes. Old calligraphic paintings, old dishes, old cameras, old phonographs, sewing machines, sculptures, bracelets, necklaces… The street was full of all kinds of antique objects that seemed to have woken up from a long sleep and somehow made their way out from under the layers of dust that had accumulated over time.

From among the antique objects that filled up the alley, making it look much narrower than it was, came an elegant melody played on a string instrument that Haruko had never heard before, and its rhythm snaked around her feet. A pipa with red tassels, a young Chinese girl in a *qipao*, an instrument with snapped strings and a broken body… These images appeared in her mind and disappeared.

She'd heard that China's antique market had many objects that Qing officials had used and discarded. Someone had purchased something among the objects that had seemed like trash but turned out to be a rare treasure. She'd even heard a somewhat exaggerated story of a chamber pot used by Empress Dowager Cixi being found in some antique market.

Haruko was illiterate and completely ignorant when it came to antiques, but now that she was at the market she wanted to buy something. She wanted to get something as a souvenir from her trip to China for her grandfather, who loved to collect old things.

As she looked around, something caught her eye. It was a wooden pipe. This smoking pipe was exactly like the one that was always stuck between her grandfather's lips—the pipe that seemed like a small hammer at first glance, the pipe that her grandfather always held in his mouth, even empty due to the doctor's relentless insistence to give up smoking to improve his asthma.

"This pipe is older than you," he'd said. "Even older than your mother."

Haruko recalled the image of the wooden pipe that her grandfather treasured. Like a polished bone, it was shiny from the touch of the hand of the heavy smoker who had owned it, and there were traces of Chinese characters etched on its worn body. There were two letters, one of which seemed like the Chinese character for gold (金), and the other was illegible as most of the strokes had been worn down. But unlike her grandfather's pipe, she could clearly see the two Chinese characters etched on the body of this one.

When she'd asked what the word etched on the pipe meant, her grandfather had never given her a straight answer, changing the topic of conversation. Thinking of her grandfather, Haruko picked up the pipe.

"Korean, you? This pipe, good antique."

The vendor, who seemed to be in his fifties and was holding an enameled cup in one hand as befitting an antique vendor, spoke in broken Korean, mistaking Haruko for a Korean.

Since she didn't know how to speak Chinese, Haruko asked about the price of the pipe in English.

Taking a sip of tea from the cup, the vendor held up his right hand with his thumb and forefinger stretched out.

In Korean, he said, "Eight hundred yuan."

A look of confusion appeared on Haruko's face, as she couldn't understand him.

"No Korean?" the vendor asked and repeated, "Eight hundred yuan, eight hundred yuan."

Haruko took out her wallet. She wanted to ask for the price by showing him the money. But she took out Japanese yen by mistake. It was a thousand-yen bill with the picture of Natsume Soseki on the front. All the Chinese yuan she and Jonghyeok had exchanged were in his wallet.

The vendor noticed the bill in Haruko's hand and crumpled his face.

"Are you Japanese?"

Although the vendor asked her in Chinese, Haruko understood his question and answered, "Yes. I'm not Korean. I'm Japanese."

Thinking that the vendor might understand Japanese, she told him that she was Japanese. Then she held out the money in her hand.

"I don't have any Chinese money," she said. "Do you take yen by any chance?"

The vendor asked again, "What? Japan?"

Then without even waiting for her answer, he snatched the pipe away from Haruko's hand.

"*Bu mai, bu mai le* (I'm not selling, not selling)!"

The vendor's voice was louder than necessary, and other vendors nearby craned their necks to look his way.

"What's going on, Old Wang?" asked one of the vendors.

"She says she's Japanese," the vendor called Old Wang answered as he scanned Haruko up and down.

"Why did a Japanese woman come to Nanjing of all places?" muttered a vendor from across the street through his teeth.

"Indeed."

"Where does she think she is, putting on airs here? That Jap!"

Other vendors spoke up as well.

Haruko didn't know what they were saying, but she could tell that they were all talking about her in an offensive way.

Putting the pipe back in its place, the vendor grumbled, "Hell, I'd rather use my precious antiques as dog bowls rather than sell them to a Japanese! I'd never sell to her first cousin, second cousin, or even third cousin!"

He took a sip of his tea once more. He rolled it around in his mouth and spat it out in a stream like water from a water pistol. It nearly splashed Haruko's skirt. Startled, she took a step back. Then she staggered. Someone caught her hand right.

"Where have you been? I told you to wait. I looked everywhere for you."

It was Jonghyeok.

Haruko stood still in Jonghyeok's embrace. The train station was full of people waiting for the express train to Shanghai. Haruko and Jonghyeok stood leaning against one another in front of the ticket booth, waiting for their train.

"It'll be okay. It's only two hours from here to Shanghai on an express train. We'll get there soon. Let's go and watch the bustling night scene of the Huangpu River and eat something delicious."

Jonghyeok caressed Haruko's weakly cowering shoulders.

"It'll be a change of scenery," he whispered softly into her ear, understanding how she was feeling inside.

After the tour of the memorial hall, Jonghyeok and Haruko parted ways with the coalition in the evening. The group was scheduled to stay in China for another week. Their goal was to research and learn about all the cases of comfort women they could across China. Promising to stay in touch with the coalition, Jonghyeok left with Haruko to head to Shanghai.

At the station, he took something out of his pocket and handed it to her. Haruko's eyes widened at the object in her hand. It was the wooden pipe.

Jonghyeok asked, "You were trying to buy this pipe earlier, right?"

"Yeah, yes," Haruko answered and bowed her head to Jonghyeok. "*Arigatou!*"

She repeated her thanks several times, holding the pipe close to her chest. She was thankful that Jonghyeok had appeared like her savior when she'd been trapped in the market under the Chinese vendors' hostile gazes, and she was even more grateful that he'd managed to purchase the gift she wanted to get for her grandfather.

"No need to thank me," Jonghyeok said. "I should be the one apologizing, actually. You came all the way to China for a fun vacation, but I've only stressed you out."

Feeling sad, Haruko inched closer to him, and Jonghyeok hugged her tightly from behind to comfort her. Haruko nestled into Jonghyeok's warm embrace without caring whether people might stare at them. Over these past few days, Haruko had felt smothered in alternating shock, guilt, and incomprehensible sorrow.

Right at that moment, a cell phone rang, splitting the two of them apart with its startling volume. It was the song "Snow Flower" by the famous Japanese singer, Mika Nakashima. Haruko had set the song as Jonghyeok's ringtone.

All eyes were suddenly on the two of them. Many had cell phones with them, but the uniquely Japanese song must have irritated their ears because they were giving annoyed looks. Hurriedly, Jonghyeok answered the phone. Then his face turned pale. After hanging up, he spoke, looking completely at a loss.

"I'm sorry, Haruko, but we have to cancel our tickets to

Shanghai."

"*Doushite* (why)?"

With his eyes welled up with tears, Jonghyeok said,
"Grandma passed away."

Cats Cry for Spring

Grandma's remains were scattered by the mass grave at the entrance of the village, as she'd requested. She'd said that the remains of her own mother—Kkeutsun— had been scattered there as well. The grave that attested to Grandma's story about the tragedy at Deer Valley was now encircled by stones and marked by a granite gravestone with the words "Historical Site of the Deer Valley Tragedy."

After leading the funeral, Jonghyeok's mother picked azaleas alongside other villagers to lay on the grave. Pink and red azalea branches covered his grandmother's ashes. Jonghyeok's grandmother and her mother would now meet again in the netherworld, full of azalea blossoms. With thick accents and loud voices, they would tell all the stories they hadn't had a chance to tell each other.

In the meantime, the azaleas were in full bloom in Deer Valley. The mountain was ablaze with pink and red azaleas, but no one had the luxury to appreciate their beauty.

Steeped in the sorrow of having lost his grandmother, Jonghyeok didn't have time to admire the flowers either, and against the backdrop of a funeral procession, azalea blossoms looked plaintive.

During the process of cremating Grandma in the city, returning to Deer Valley with her remains for the funeral attended by the townspeople, scattering the remains by the town entrance, and heading back home, Jonghyeok's mother was mired in sadness. Jonghyeok and Haruko stood by her the entire time. Having held a job for a long time, Jonghyeok's mother seemed stylish and much younger than her age, but she was a woman in her seventies, and she was completely exhausted. Sorrow weighed her down even more.

"It was an auspicious death, since she was well into her nineties."

"It's true. No one could ever accuse her of being heartless during her lifetime. She led a good life. And she's enjoyed the long life that the heavens had given her, so it is an auspicious death," the elderly people from the village remarked as they drank up the wine from the funeral rite and ate the well-prepared food.

But Jonghyeok's mother shook her head from side to side in sadness. With tears welled up in her eyes, she poured the funeral rite wine into people's cups as she said, "There's no such thing as an auspicious death when it's your own parent."

She said she just felt sad, guilty, and heartbroken.

Elderly townspeople offered words of consolation, but Jonghyeok's mother couldn't take them in. Even the end of Grandma's life was too heartrending and wretched, like the unimaginably cruel and thorny path she'd had to walk her entire life.

After offering a drink of wine to each and every elderly person at the funeral, Jonghyeok's mother poured herself a cup and drank it. The strong wine stung her throat and touched part of her pained heart. She spun around to a corner and burst into tears again. Jonghyeok approached her and put his arms around her. Leaning into her son's firm shoulders, she became even more mournful and her sobs grew louder.

With her eyes sunken deep like potholes, Jonghyeok's

mother spoke in a moan, "I washed and dressed your grandmother after she passed, and… and I noticed that she had a big scar below her breasts. When I looked closer, the scar was Chinese characters. Her body was scrawny thin, but the letters were there without having faded even a little bit. It was a name in Japanese."

Jonghyeok's mother shuddered as she spoke, and Jonghyeok could feel the vibrations of her body.

He also noticed Haruko's ashen face, as she sat quietly in one corner of the room, watching Jonghyeok and his mother. Without realizing, she'd become a member of the deceased's family, and her face reflected the pain and fatigue that was on the faces of the bereaved family. Moreover, having vividly heard Grandma's testimony by her side, Haruko felt her sorrow dig deep and hard into her heart.

Even in the car on the way back home after Grandma's funeral, Jonghyeok's mother sat, detached, in his arms. Jonghyeok supported her delicate body with his shoulders. Haruko's nervously wavering eyes reflected in the rearview mirror.

Jonghyeok's mother, who had been letting her body sway to the rhythm of the car's movements, suddenly opened her eyes wide. Then she spoke in a loud voice as though she'd been possessed.

"My goodness, the cats… I didn't even remember…"

Reminded of the cats, Jonghyeok exclaimed aloud as well, "Oh no, we forgot the cats!"

Jonghyeok and Haruko opened the door carefully. They lifted it up a little bit and pushed. The slanted old door with worn down hinges creaked open. Grandma had passed away even before Jonghyeok could get the door fixed. The creaks from the hinges sounded like sad moans. Feeling an ache in his heart, Jonghyeok froze for a moment with his hand still gripping the door handle. He felt like Grandma would greet him any moment now, saying, "Goodness, you're here, Jonghyeok!" in her wheezy voice.

She had been a generous grandmother, who'd pick cucumbers from her vegetable garden and keep them cold in a water jar to give him, who'd give him rice cakes and candies from her pockets like a magician on days she'd been to a feast or celebration in town and watch her grandson eat with a smile beaming through her wrinkles.

She'd greeted him with a clear, high-pitched voice just

a few days before, but now her house was empty.

The *ondol* floor with yellow linoleum, framed photographs lining the walls… The deck of *hwatu* cards, shiny from grandmother's touch over the years, was placed on the warmest part of the *ondol* floor.

There was a pair of rubber shoes with their sides stretched out. The owner of those shoes was no more. When she noticed the pair of black rubber shoes, Haruko felt a pang of grief in her heart.

When the rusty door opened with a clang, there was a *meow*. The cats sat inside, protecting the house that was now bereft of Jonghyeok's grandmother. They'd been crouching scattered about the room when they heard the noises that Jonghyeok and Haruko made, and they stared with their ears pricked up.

Jonghyeok picked up a spotted one from the floor and held it in his arms. He stroked the feline's round head. The cat rounded its back and nuzzled in his arms. Jonghyeok looked around at the roomful of cats with a warm gaze.

"I'm sorry," he quietly murmured. "We almost forgot you. Grandma loved you cats when she was alive…"

His voice was thick with tears.

Haruko picked up one of the cats as well. It was a plain-looking one that was clearly shabbier-looking than the expensive Japanese Bobtails her grandfather had in Matsuyama. Yet this countryside farm cat had affection hidden beneath its plainness. She could feel the soft cat's warmth nestled in her arms. She stroked its fluffy coat.

Jonghyeok looked closely around the room to count the felines, afraid that some might have disappeared while he was wallowing in sadness during his grandmother's funeral.

"All six of them are here. Thank goodness."

Hearing the voice and feeling the warmth of humans, the cats began to gather one by one around the warmest spot in the room.

"Sunhwa, Gwang-ok, Okbun, Yeongsin, Hye-ok, Malja…"

Jonghyeok called the names of the cats as he gave them sausage pieces he'd brought in his pockets. But the cats stared at him without touching the sausages. One of them sat still without budging even a little bit on the warm floor where Grandma had often lain on her side.

Suddenly Haruko shuddered. Something like a flash of lightning struck her. As if it noticed the change in

Haruko's emotions, the cat in her arms looked up at her.

Meow! The cat opened its blossom-like mouth and let out a cry.

Unable to look into the cat's black, jade-like eyes, Haruko looked elsewhere.

She uttered, "I just realized… all the cats were … named after other comfort women."

Jonghyeok nodded. Haruko could see that his glasses were fogging up from the dew that seeped out of the corners of his eyes. Haruko covered her mouth with her hand. She couldn't hold back the sobs that surged up inside her. With the cat still in her arms, Haruko stood facing the cupboards. She could see the portrait of Grandma placed inside the glass-pane cupboard.

Wearing white mourning clothes and with her hair neatly pulled up in a bun with a hairpin, she looked well-kept and elegant in her portrait, though it had been taken for the purpose of her funeral.

Jonghyeok's mother had had the new *hanbok* tailor-made for Grandma and had taken her to a photo studio in the city for this picture, which would be attached to the documents that needed to be submitted to the Home Affairs Bureau. Saying it had come out very well, she had the photograph enlarged and printed, and hung it on the wall.

But now that beautiful photograph had black ribbons around it.

Haruko felt the tip of her nose sting and her lips twitch as she tried to hold back tears. Then she fell to her knees in front of Grandma's photograph, repeating inarticulate words through her tears.

"*Obaasan, gomenasai* (grandmother, I'm sorry)…"

Monochrome Memories

The van arrived at a small house in the county seat. During the winter holidays, Jonghyeok once again spent his time with the members of the Coalition for Comfort Women Issues. He participated in the investigation of Korean comfort women in China and volunteered as a Chinese-Korean interpreter.

His trip back home in the spring had given him another task. Even as he stayed up all night for his doctoral defense, he busied himself collecting data and sources on the remaining comfort women in China. While straining under the burden of busy academic work, he dedicated himself to contacting Chinese researchers studying comfort women and amassing relevant information.

But on this trip, Haruko was nowhere to be seen.

On one spring day, after they returned to Tokyo from the trip to Jonghyeok's hometown, the two of them met at the restaurant Akamon by the university's front gate. Jonghyeok thought that Haruko chose the noodle house for some comfort food after having to eat unagreeable foreign food for so long, but when he sat across from her, Haruko opened her mouth and the words that flowed out were a huge shock to Jonghyeok.

"Jonghyeok-*ssi*," Haruko addressed him formally and paused in a moment of hesitation.

As he placed a spoon and chopsticks on Haruko's side of the table, Jonghyeok looked over at Haruko with concern. She was looking extremely serious, and she was speaking Korean.

Haruko only spoke Korean in two cases—when she turned on her charm and wanted Jonghyeok to praise her for her fluency or when she wanted to discuss something serious that she didn't want people nearby to hear.

"I think we have to break up," she said in Korean.

Without a word, Jonghyeok placed the container of seasoning in front of Haruko in an orderly fashion.

"We have to break up," Haruko repeated. She

enunciated every syllable.

The bowls of ramen arrived at the table just then. Haruko paused for a moment in front of the heaps of ramen noodles submerged in hot, steamy broth.

"*Oishii* (yummy)!" Jonghyeok let out an exaggerated exclamation in Japanese and shoveled the noodles into his mouth.

During their trip he'd had as much of the food from home as he wanted, but he did miss the spicy Akamon ramen during his trip home. Haruko also ate without a word.

While slurping the noodles into his mouth, he suddenly stopped moving his spoon and looked across the table at Haruko. Tears were falling into her ramen bowl as she bowed her head and ate the ramen.

"*Nazeda* (why are you crying)?" asked Jonghyeok. "Are you feeling sick?"

Haruko shook her head from side to side.

"Did I do something wrong?"

She shook her head again.

Not only were her big, deep-set eyes full of unease, but she was also avoiding Jonghyeok's gaze, unlike her usual self.

343

After pulling out a tissue to dab her lips, Haruko began to speak.

"I actually did think a lot about things like the Nanjing Massacre and comfort women when I started dating an ethnic Korean from China. I looked up a lot of expert opinions to find answers as to why Japan should be held accountable for the issue and how the post-war Japanese government and Japanese people should take responsibility for it. I did it without telling you. These were issues that were mentioned every day in China, Korea, and Japan, and I'd never really given them much thought before—before I met you, I mean…"

Haruko fidgeted with the soup spoon in her hand as she continued, "And during this trip, I realized that I'm one of those people who can no longer ignore these questions."

Haruko kept on talking in Korean. Couples eating ramen at nearby tables glanced at the two of them as they spoke soberly in a foreign language.

"And your answer to those questions is to flee?" Jonghyeok asked in an extremely gentle yet pleading voice, looking for an answer.

Haruko lifted her head. She stared into Jonghyeok's

face. As he looked into her burning eyes welled up with tears, Jonghyeok felt like he could tell what her eyes were trying to say.

"Is it possible... for the grandson of a comfort woman forced to service the Japanese military to love—of all people—a Japanese woman?"

After asking this question out loud, Haruko stood up from the table. She scurried over to the counter. Her footsteps faltered a little.

"Are you breaking up with your boyfriend?" the plump lady at the counter smiled and asked jokingly, without realizing what had happened between the two of them. "Why else would a girl pay for the meal?"

Afraid that she might burst into tears, Haruko kept her head bowed as she pulled money out of her wallet. Without a word, she took out a bill with the picture of Natsume Soseki and paid for the ramen. Then she bowed deep, perhaps to the lady at the counter or to Jonghyeok, and ran out of the shop.

Jonghyeok waited for Haruko's dimpled face to appear behind the window of the noodle shop. He waited for her to press her face against the window and wave her hand at him like a cat figurine. But her face never appeared.

Jonghyeok looked over at the *maneki-neko*, the cat figurine that was supposed to bring luck, sitting on the counter. The battery-powered figurine used to swing its forepaw at the guests, but it was stationary today. Jonghyeok picked up his spoon from the table, then put it back down. His ramen noodles had gone cold.

They had gotten into spats because of their drastic cultural differences. But they'd subconsciously avoided head-on confrontation, and so those spats never lasted. Jonghyeok had been careful to avoid sensitive topics and embraced his young and beautiful girlfriend.

Once they'd had a serious conversation about Ahn Jung-geun. Jonghyeok had the literary journal *Shakai Bungaku* (Social Literature), published by the Association for Japanese Social Literature, open to the first page of a paper and stabbed at it with his forefinger.

Then he enunciated the title: "The Shadow of National Ideology Cast Over Natsume Soseki's Novel *The Gate*."

Befuddled, Haruko stared at Jonghyeok out of curiosity.

"This paper says that Ahn Jung-geun's assassination of Ito Hirobumi had a huge impact on Natsume Soseki's literary works," said Jonghyeok excitedly. "Soseki's *The Gate* was serialized in *The Asahi Shimbun* from March 1 to June 12, 1910, which was when Ahn Jung-geun was in jail awaiting execution. As you know, *The Gate* is one of Natsume Soseki's major novels, alongside *Sanshiro* and *Then*."

Jonghyeok was so enthusiastic about the paper that he'd nearly memorized it.

"The novel tells the love story of a poor and young married couple in Tokyo and comments on an individual's love and social ethics. But there's something more noteworthy. At the beginning of the novel, there's the mention of the assassination of Ito Hirobumi. The protagonist couple's discussion of the reasons for the killing is described in detail. And the plot involves the protagonist being betrayed by his friends and family and roaming through Manchuria afterward, where Ito was assassinated. This critic says that Manchuria as a symbol of Japanese aggression and Manchuria as a symbol of the protagonist's immoral past overlap in this novel."

Without even waiting to see Haruko's reaction, Jonghyeok rattled on, "Some critics argued that the character Yasui is actually based on Ahn Jung-geun, from the Chinese character of his name '安,' which is 'An' in Korean. And when you think about it, *The Gate* does project the Meiji government's ideology, which was heading toward militarism. Until now, Japanese academia has consciously avoided connecting Soseki's works and Ahn Jung-geun's noble deed, but according to this paper Japanese scholars have recently been acknowledging such a connection.

"What are your thoughts on this, Haruko?" he asked as he glanced over at her.

Haruko answered thoughtfully, "When it comes to history, the relationship between China and Japan and that between Korea and Japan tend to become tense. Both parties make an effort to be on good terms, but it's like a tangled knot that is difficult to undo. We can't do much about what has already happened, but I believe that what's more important is the process of handling and addressing the past and apologizing for it. I'm sorry to say but our generation isn't much aware of the past deeds that the previous generation committed. We only remember that Ahn Jung-geun is a hero admired by South Korea and that Soseki is a writer respected by Japan. From your perspective, Ahn is a respectable man, but he's been imprinted in our collective memory as a terrorist. I once thought hard about Ahn Jung-geun. I was really surprised to learn that he was a pacifist who wanted peace in the East, and that he sought ways for Korea, China, and Japan to establish a joint bank and military over a hundred years ago.

"Once my classmates asked me what my boyfriend thought of Ahn Jung-geun. To them, I'm the outsider who dates an ethnic Korean from China, of all things. They got mad at me then because I didn't say anything, but because of them I got to learn more about Ahn."

Haruko's voice was imbued with the helplessness and bitterness of having become a social outsider for dating a non-Japanese man. Jonghyeok couldn't possibly continue the serious conversation.

But things were different this time. As they listened to Jonghyeok's grandmother's blood-curdling testimony, and as they toured the Nanjing Massacre Memorial Hall and the former comfort stations, Jonghyeok and Haruko both detected a coldness, like the chill in the air before the frost. What had been a snippy chill that made the two of them shiver had turned into an unstoppable cold front that created icebergs and chasms between them.

Neither brought up the topics that were like landmines, landmines that would go off when touched, something that would incur the wrath of God, yet both were suffering from their own agonies, swept up by the storm clouds that surrounded these topics.

After their last supper of tearful ramen, Haruko severed all ties with Jonghyeok. She didn't take his calls or answer his emails. Then, a few days later, she'd changed her phone number.

The van squeezed into the alley and stopped in front of a shabby mudbrick house.

"Around here, in the village of Shimenzi (石門子), there was a Japanese military camp and a comfort station within the camp grounds."

People from the city branch of the All-China Women's Federation and the Home Affairs Bureau welcomed them and told them about the traces of comfort women discovered in the area. Jonghyeok translated their words into Korean for the members of the Coalition for Comfort Women Issues.

In her testimony, Grandma had mentioned the Chinese character for rock "石" in the name of the place she was transported to, and Jonghyeok wondered if this was it. After a short meeting in the office of the women's association, the party arrived at the house of a newly discovered comfort woman.

Past the empty front yard, they reached the dwelling. On the door was a sticker with the Chinese character for blessing written upside down. A corner of it had come loose and was fluttering in the wind. When someone pushed the door open, the muggy and stuffy air mixed with exhaust fumes that had pooled inside the house rushed out and enveloped the visitors.

The mudbrick walls weren't even limewashed, and they were stained with soot and what seemed like rat piss here and there. The small window was covered with layers of plastic, making the entire house dark despite the bright daylight outside.

An elderly lady who had been lying under the blanket on the high *ondol* floor slowly sat up.

"This is Ms. Li Guang-yu," a staff member from the women's association introduced the old lady to the group, then sat down on the *ondol* by her side and spoke loudly into her ear.

"These people came from Korea. They came to hear

your story."

The elderly lady patted down her hair as white as leek roots. She groped along the wall with her hands and then pulled on a cord to turn on the light. A lightbulb stained with dried-up fly specks lit up.

The silhouette of the elderly lady sitting with her back to the window came into view under the naked light, and the moment he laid his eyes on her, Jonghyeok blushed and tears welled up in his eyes.

She was wearing a sleeveless jacket that had lost all its buttons, and what held her hair bun together on the back of her head was not a hairpin but an old toothbrush with worn-down bristles. The elderly lady smiled, showing her shrunken and discolored gums. And in the next moment, everyone froze in their spot. It wasn't because the conditions of her house were terrible. And it wasn't because they didn't see a single tooth when she opened her caved mouth.

"*Huanying, huanying* (welcome, welcome)."

It was because she greeted them in fluent Chinese. She didn't speak a word of Korean.

She flailed her arms and grabbed the visitors' hands in hers. Even at a glance, her thick and rough fingers told them of the years of hardship she'd lived through. But there was power in her liver-spotted hands. With them, she grasped everyone's hand for a while, holding onto and patting them.

Like a student waiting to be called on, the old lady sat and listened to the Women's Federation members and the coalition's team leader explain why they came to see her. After swallowing hard, she finally began to speak.

Forgetting to press the shutter of the camera he held in his hand, Jonghyeok stared at the old woman. He'd flown to China on his own and joined the Coalition for Comfort Women Issues as soon as he'd heard that they had found someone presumed to be the Gwang-ok mentioned in Grandma's testimony in Dongning County, Heilongjiang Province. She was Chunja's cousin, who jumped off the truck transporting the comfort women in the middle of the night and hid in the forest.

But this lady didn't speak a word of Korean. That made everyone wonder whether she really was a Korean comfort woman. Then Jonghyeok remembered that the Israelites had nearly forgotten their language after centuries of nomadic life without a country. Everyone said that it was possible that she had forgotten Korean because she hadn't spoken it for eighty years. Moreover, because she'd spent her entire life within the walls of unfamiliar despair, yoked by the burden of pain, without a single person to talk to in Korean.

But she can't even speak a single word in Korean? Jonghyeok was sad and disappointed.

Chewing on her lips with her toothless gums and wringing her hands like the branches of an old tree, the old lady recalled her memories of the past. As if possessed, she began to speak.

Her quiet and gentle face certainly was that of a typical Korean grandmother, but a strong northeastern Chinese accent poured out of her every time she opened her mouth. It came as a shock to everyone there. All the people who sat around her quietly wiped tears from their eyes. Jonghyeok had a hard time focusing the camera on her face because of his own misty eyes.

According to her testimony, her parents opened an inn by a river across from which you could see Korea, and the year she'd turned sixteen she left home when she was recruited to work at a Japanese textile factory but ended up as a comfort woman at a military camp. There was a well in the camp, and she said the corpses of comfort women were dumped in that well. Unable to endure satisfying the soldiers' carnal desires, she jumped off a moving truck in the middle of the night, and she took a bullet in her shoulder when the soldiers shot at her.

Without reserve, she took off her top in front of everyone, revealing her pale and scrawny radish-like torso. Under her left collarbone, there was a round scar, black as though the blood from back then remained clotted even today. The bullet had remained in her body, and her shoulder ached on rainy days. Just twenty years ago, she'd learned that the bullet was still inside her when she'd gone to the hospital after feeling weak, and she'd had it taken out.

With her back bent forward, the old lady crawled over to the orange-painted wardrobe and took out an envelope. It contained an x-ray. The staff member of the women's association took it and held it up to the lightbulb. All eyes shifted to the x-ray. It was an image of a torso so thin that it resembled the skeletal branches of trees in the winter. The white bullet the size of a thumb was clearly stuck in her shoulder.

"Among the people who were taken by the Japanese military with you, was there a cousin your age?" asked

Jonghyeok.

The old lady put her hand by her ear. The staff member of the Women's Federation repeated his words in a voice that was an octave higher.

"He's asking if you had a cousin, ma'am."

Her voice was loud as though she were speaking through a megaphone.

"She's a bit hard of hearing," said the staff member with an embarrassed smile. There was something like melancholy ingrained in her voice.

The old lady stared at Jonghyeok. She mumbled something through her caved-in mouth. She was struggling to restore colors to her hazy, monochrome memories.

Jonghyeok took out his laptop. He turned it on and clicked open the video file of his grandmother's testimony. Chewing on her lips with her toothless gums, the old lady looked closely at Grandma Chunja on the screen. In the video, old Chunja began to sing:

From every stormy wind that blows,
From every swelling tide of woes,
There is a calm, a sure retreat—

'Tis found beneath the mercy seat.

She was singing the psalm she'd learned from the bachelor teacher Jang Mo-se.

As the old lady watched the screen, her eyes wavered. She began to move her lips quickly. Then out of the blue she began to sing.

There is a scene where spirits blend,
Where friend holds fellowship with friend…

She clapped as she continued:
Though sundered far, by faith they meet
Around one common mercy seat…

The old lady on the screen and the old lady who was watching the old lady on the screen both clapped their hands as they sang in unison:

From every stormy wind that blows,
From every swelling tide of woes…

The old lady's face crumpled up like a piece of paper.

From the corners of her narrowed eyes, tears trickled down like pine sap. She then held up her forefinger and pointed at the screen. Her nail-less digit shook like a buoy bobbing up and down in the ocean. Barely managing to swallow the sorrow that seemed to clog up her throat like phlegm, she started to shout at the top of her lungs as if she were shouting an alarm.

"Chunja! Chunja!"

A Sturdy Pipe

The tea kettle was boiling. Kneeling in front of the tea table, Haruko stared at the kettle. Under the table, several cats sat crouched and perfectly still, as if they were in an ukiyo-e painting. Haruko scooped tea leaves with a spoon and placed them in the kettle. Then she waited for the tea to brew.

She picked up one of the cats sitting by her feet and scratched its head as she held it in her arms. As she looked around at her grandfather's cats, she thought of the other felines she'd recently seen. She recalled their names one by one: Sunhwa, Gwang-ok, Okbun, Yeongsin, Hye-ok, Malja…

The names came to her so vividly that Haruko shivered.

Out of habit, she took out her cell phone and opened

the Kakao Talk app. There was another message from Jonghyeok.

Since she'd broken up with him at the ramen shop, Jonghyeok had come to her dormitory to see her several times and called her even more, but Haruko never answered the calls or met with him. She eventually changed her phone number. Haruko knew well that Jonghyeok was going through the most difficult time in his life and that she should be there to share his pain. But knowing that the weight of the pain that pressed down on his shoulders was nothing other than their own past, she couldn't come up with a way to help him, and she had to swallow her shame.

Then they happened to run into each other by the Sanshiro Pond made famous in Natsume Soseki's novel, where they'd met for the first time. With gaunt eyes, Jonghyeok said he'd waited for Haruko to pass by for days.

Yet Haruko once again refused Jonghyeok's touch.

"Would it be possible… for the grandson of a comfort woman forced to service the Japanese military to love—of all people—a Japanese woman?" Haruko repeated those same words. She then answered her own question, "It cannot be."

At that moment, Jonghyeok's footsteps that had quickly followed after her stopped.

"I'll wait until you think things over. I can wait forever."

She could hear Jonghyeok's voice fade behind her. The moment his steps stopped chasing her, Haruko felt like her heart also stopped. Afraid that he might see her tears, she quickly walked off the school campus.

After that day, Haruko tried to pull herself together and focus on her studies. Jonghyeok must have given up as well because she didn't hear from him at all. But then one day, after really a long time, he sent her a message through Kakao Talk.

"They discovered a new haiku written by Natsume Soseki. This haiku he'd written in a letter to a colleague at Jinjo Middle School in Ehime Prefecture, where he worked before he was assigned to teach at Kumamoto High School, was apparently found at the house belonging to a relative of that colleague… Jinjo Middle School is the one that appears in Soseki's *Botchan*. The haiku was part of a letter to Ikai Takehiko, who taught literature at Jinjo Middle School. He'd written the letter when he moved to a different region. It seems that Soseki was a really considerate person."

Jonghyeok had often enjoyed talking about his research area. In the next message, he added that he would send her a haiku when he couldn't bear how much he missed her.

Haiku is a type of short-form poetry in Japan. A modern form of poetry rooted in *haikai renga* verses, haikus were created by taking the first verses of *renga*, which were composed by multiple poets exchanging alternating stanzas and became established as a form of literary art. Often composed on the spot, haikus require a quick wit and pithy responses.

It began hundreds of years ago, and now there are millions of writers who specialized exclusively in haikus in Japan alone. Today, haikus aren't just a Japanese literary genre. More and more writers in the United States and Europe write them in their own languages.

Starting that day, Jonghyeok sent her a haiku nearly every day.

On the day he saw a butterfly, he sent her a haiku by Moritake:

A fallen blossom
Returning to the bough, I thought –
But no, a butterfly.[4]

On a rainy day with a thunderstorm, he sent her a haiku by Basho:

How admirable!
To see lightning and not think
Life is fleeting.[5]

One night with a bright, full moon, he sent her one by Sokan:

O Moon! - if we
Should put a handle to you
What a fan you'd be![6]

Around the times seasons changed, he sent her haikus about seasons, written by Buson, Issa, and Basho:

I go,
You stay;

Two autumns.[7]

Quite remarkable
Being born human…
Autumn dusk.[8]

Has it returned,
The snow
We viewed together?[9]

With the news of the passing of one of the comfort women, he sent her Soseki's haiku:

Breathing pauses in the
Monk's chant for the dead:
Grasshopper's chirp.[10]

And when the spring came again, he sent one by Basho:

First day of spring—
I keep thinking about
the end of autumn.[11]

The form of a Haiku is short, but the mind pictures they paint are vast. Every day, Jonghyeok conveyed his feelings and thoughts to Haruko through haikus.

After the tea in the kettle finished boiling, Haruko poured it into the teacups. The dense fragrance of the tea spread throughout the room, and her grandfather let out a short grunt. The pointy ends of his Kaiser mustache twitched.

One of the cats got up and slinked over to Grandpa. Haruko quickly picked it up into her arms.

"Kitty, no. Grandpa's ill."

As she stroked the cat's round head, she looked over at her grandfather with eyes full of concern.

A few months ago, he'd collapsed from a stroke. Her clever and eloquent grandfather was now unable to move by himself. His speech was slurred as though he had a piece of candy in his mouth. His age-defying, commanding presence had faded, leaving only a handful of stiff bones and flesh. He was shorter, and his eccentricity turned into extreme sensitivity such that he became prone to crumpling up his wan face like a sheet of paper and spitting out unintelligible profanities.

Haruko opened the kettle lid. She then picked up the

kettle with a cotton cloth and poured the tea into teacups. After waiting for the hot liquid to cool a bit, Haruko picked up the teacup and a short straw and brought them both to her grandfather. She stuck the straw into the teacup and let the tea that had cooled down enough flow into the corner of Grandpa's mouth. Her mother had told her to give him cooled tea frequently as his mouth kept going dry, before she left for a little while.

Grandpa waved his gnarly hands like a blind man waving a stick in front of him. At his strong refusal, Haruko realized, albeit too late, that she'd brewed pu-erh tea. Several times she'd given him the Chinese tea and he'd spat it out. Even though he was drifting in and out of consciousness, his refusal was strong.

"Wasn't tea originally discovered by Shennong and introduced to Japan? That's what it says in *The Classic of Tea*, written by Lu Yu from the Tang Dynasty. It says that the very first human to drink tea was Yan Emperor Shennong, five thousand years ago. Isn't that true, lady who studied the 'way of the tea'?"

That was what Jonghyeok had said when she'd told him that Grandpa didn't drink the Chinese pu-erh tea, after their unexpected encounter with him.

Neither Jonghyeok nor Haruko could understand Grandpa's stubborn rejection of Chinese products.

"We're out of other tea, Grandpa," Haruko said to her grandfather. "Mother will bring the *gyokuro* green tea that you like when she comes back in the evening, so until then, at least have some of this Chinese tea."

Grandpa could tell the smell of pu-erh tea from a mile away. Even though Haruko explained to him that the Qing emperor Jianlong drank the tea and lived a long life, or that the tea was great for asthma, the old man still refused it. He insisted on only drinking the Japanese *gyokuro* tea, although Haruko doubted that he could taste the subtle differences between well-brewed tea and regular tea in his state.

Grandpa stubbornly shook his white head from side to side. Watching him, Haruko recalled the story of the phrase "soseki chinryu (漱石枕流)" that Jonghyeok had told her once.

It was a story recorded in *The Book of Jin*, where a boastful and impudent young man named Sun Chu expressed his wish to become a recluse to his friend Wang ji by saying, "I will rinse my mouth with rocks and pillow my head on the running stream (漱石枕流, soseki

367

chinryu)," when what he actually meant was "I will pillow my head on rocks and rinse my mouth in the running stream (枕石漱流, chinseki soryu)."

Noticing Sun Chu's slip of the tongue, Wang Ji asked, "Why would you rinse your mouth with rocks and pillow your head on the running stream?"

Sun Chu realized his mistake then, but he pressed on and said, "I will pillow my head on the running stream to cleanse my ears of the useless noises of the world, and I will rinse my mouth with rocks to make my teeth even stronger!"

The phrase "soseki chinryu" referred to how forcing a situation in an attempt to cover up a mistake ends up revealing one's true nature—it was an adage about the importance of admitting and apologizing for your mistakes.

Jonghyeok said that he'd only learned about this phrase while studying Natsume Soseki. The author was actually born Natsume Kinnosuke, but he adopted Sosuke as his penname from the phrase "soseki chinryu."

Soseki had changed his name in defiance of his family's complicated history and the world, but Grandpa was as obstinate as Sun Chu.

Upon hearing that Haruko had been to China with Jonghyeok, Grandpa had taken the last train from Dogo Onsen and rushed to Tokyo to see her. As he listened to Haruko talk about her trip, his face had turned ashen.

"Are you insane? How could you possibly follow that Chinaman there of all places? You *merou* (foolish girl)!"

Grandpa, who had always called her "Onsen Princess," had called her a bad name for the first time, and Haruko had stood up to him for the first time. She emphatically told him at the top of her lungs about the comfort women, the Nanjing Massacre, and the war of catastrophes that Japan brought down on Asia. He had stared at her with a look she'd never seen on his face before. Then he spoke with a hoarse voice thick with phlegm.

"We went to war with the weight of the peace of the East on our shoulders. We were even younger than you are now. There is no one today who would give their lives for our country as we did with all our heart, and that's the problem."

Haruko raised her eyes and asked him the question that she'd longed to ask, "So dragging young women from ordinary households and killing innocent people were all for the peace of the East?"

369

"Stop this nonsense!"

Grandpa had picked up the cane he'd placed down by his side and slammed it down on the table.

"You're taking what the world says at face value?" he exclaimed. "You senseless and foolish girl…"

His Kaiser mustache twitched. Grabbing his cane, he rose from his seat and announced, "I'm going home!"

Haruko's mother quickly chased after him and stopped him.

"How are you going to go home this late in the day?"

"Move!" said Grandpa as he stood by the door with his hands on his cane. "It was a holy war we waged to liberate a billion people of the East from the hands of the Anglo-Saxons, to build the Greater East Asia Co-Prosperity Sphere without fear or favor. We readily devoted our youth and our blood for that holy war. I will never forget that time. As a man, I have never felt the true meaning of life as I did then."

After uttering those words that sounded more like mumblings, he slammed the sliding door shut and left.

"Oh, Father!"

Haruko's mother had chased after him barefoot.

A few days after the heated exchange of words with his

granddaughter, Grandpa had had a stroke.

Haruko placed a straw in Grandpa's wrinkled and twisted mouth that resembled a cavern and dripped cooled pu-erh tea into his mouth. Grandpa shook his head from side to side. He spat out the straw and the tea. His chin and neck were covered with it. He tried to brush down his wet Kaiser mustache with his right thumb, but his twisted hand didn't work the way he wanted. It was something he did out of habit to look solemn, but he couldn't even complete that small action.

As she dabbed at the tea stains with a dry towel, Haruko recalled the phrase "soseki chinryu" once again. Just then, something touched her hand. It was Grandpa's pipe placed by his head.

A small wooden pipe that resembled a handheld hammer. The pipe was as shiny as a bone, having been worn down in the hands of a chain smoker for years. The words that were etched on the pipe were nearly erased and difficult to ascertain. They were two Chinese characters— one looked like *jin* (金), the character for "gold," but the other was too faded to read. He managed to stop smoking at his doctor's urging, but he always kept the pipe between his lips out of habit. Trying hard to get some remnant of the tobacco smoke, he used to suck on the empty pipe.

"What does it say on the pipe?" Haruko used to ask, and Grandpa always evaded an answer by saying, "That pipe is older than you. Older than your mother, even."

Haruko took out another pipe from her bag. It was the one she was going to give Grandpa as a gift from her trip to China. She held the new pipe and Grandpa's old pipe in her hands and compared the two. The pipe was carved out of maple wood. They were exactly the same, as if they'd been cast in the same mold. The only difference was that one was shiny like a bone, worn down in her grandfather's hand, whereas the other still had deep wood grains, not having passed through the hands of smokers. Even the characters etched on the pipe were crystal clear, like they had only recently been inked.

The character that was faded and couldn't be read on her grandfather's pipe was *ling* (陵), meaning "hill." Together, the two characters read "Jinling."

"Do you know why the other name for Nanjing is Jinling? Jinling is a name that originated from Zhongshan Mountain, which is located to the east. In the olden days, it used to be called Mount Jinling, because during the Warring States period, when King Wu of Chu defeated the State of Yue, he noticed that there was an imperial energy surrounding the mountain. So he suppressed it by burying a golden doll in the mountains."

Haruko recalled the story about Nanjing's nickname that they had been told by Professor Zhang, who was studying the comfort women issue at Nanjing University and who had guided Jonghyeok and Haruko's party through Nanjing.

With the two pipes in her hands, Haruko hesitated for a while. Then she finally opened her mouth.

"I've heard from Father that you enlisted at a young age and fought in the war. You must have brought this pipe home as a trophy."

Grandpa struggled as he turned to face her. With one side of his mouth drooping from paralysis and his eyes sunken, he looked at Haruko. His gaze wasn't that of an adoring grandfather but a gaze full of fear, as though he were looking at a goblin with horns, holding a stick in her hand ready to bring it down on him.

Haruko lowered her eyes. And she breached the topic as if she were handling a bomb.

"You fought in the war in China."

As she struggled to utter those words, Haruko could

feel her own voice tremble.

"Hmm…" Grandpa moaned.

He reached his hand out toward Haruko. With his stiff, twisted hand, he tried to snatch the pipe in Haruko's hand. Feeling sorry to see his hand that was as skeletal as a branch of a tree during a drought, Haruko slipped the pipe into his grasp. The pipe he'd barely grabbed fell out of his hand.

He stretched his arm toward Haruko once again. Haruko again helped him grab the pipe. Grandpa slowly brought the pipe in his trembling hand to his lips and managed to put it in his mouth.

After a moment's hesitation, Haruko asked quietly, "You've also been to… Nanjing, right?"

Grandpa's lower jaw trembled, making his dentures chatter against the mouthpiece of the pipe. At the sound that resembled a woodpecker pecking away at a tree trunk in preparation for the coming of winter, Haruko felt goosebumps creep all over her skin.

The pipe fell out of Grandpa's mouth. He kept scratching the floor with his stiff claw. He was trying to pick up the pipe. Like a drowning man trying to grasp at straws, he was trying to grasp the pipe with his unyielding, trembling hand.

Haruko looked at her grandfather as if he were a stranger. At the strange sense of unfamiliarity that rose from somewhere deep inside her, she suddenly scrambled to her feet.

A cat screeched at Haruko's inadvertent kick.

"Mother will be here soon," said Haruko.

Then she ran out of the room as if she were being chased, then stopped short by the sliding door. She could hear Grandpa saying something. Thinking that he was calling for her, Haruko stopped to listen. But he wasn't calling her.

A song. He was singing. He was singing a song, though the lyrics were slurred. In the next moment, a shockwave went through Haruko's body. She knew the song he was singing. She could tell.

Iron… castles on the sea for the offense and defense… we trust in you.
Floating castles… shall… defend the Empire of the Ri… Ri…Rising Sun to the end.

As though she'd been lashed by a sudden chill, she

hugged her arms around her body. She stared at her grandfather lying on the tatami mats on the floor and the cats sitting around him like they were apparitions.

Sunhwa, Gwang-ok, Okbun, Yeongsin, Hye-ok, Malja…

The names of the cats at Deer Valley popped into her head again like the names of spirits.

Grandpa was barely managing to sing the song, his vocalization marred. The song creeped out like many-legged bugs, slowly crawled over the tatami mats, and coiled around Haruko's ankles. Haruko shuddered in horror.

Our Time

Jonghyeok disembarked the tram he'd boarded at Matsuyama. When he got off, a cute little train passed by before his eyes. It was the famous Botchan Ressha. This was the first time he'd come to Dogo Onsen in a while. The place Natsume Soseki had lauded saying, "While there was nothing in this town which compared favorably with Tokyo, the hot springs were worthy of praise"[12]; the hot springs with three thousand years of history that emperors as well as poets and artists frequented—that was where Jonghyeok found himself once again.

The last time he came, he was with Haruko, but this time he was alone. His heart felt even emptier at the thought, and Jonghyeok unwittingly let out a short sigh.

On his way to Dogo in the morning, he heard the news about the passing of another comfort woman.

"Kim Yeon-hee, one of the comfort women survivors who was forced into sexual slavery for the Japanese troops, passed away at the age of eighty-three. This brings the number of surviving comfort women to forty-nine, out of 238 registered. The Korean Council for the Women Drafted for Military Sexual Slavery by Japan announced on its official Facebook page that Ms. Kim died around 10 p.m. In 1944, Kim was a fifth grader who was assigned by her Japanese principal to go to Japan. Upon arriving at Shimonoseki, she was taken to a factory for airplane parts in Toyama Prefecture, where she worked for nine months. Then she was taken to a comfort station in Aomori Prefecture where she spent seven months as a comfort woman. She underwent treatment in a mental facility due to the trauma she experienced in the comfort station. She never married and lived alone…"

Listening to the news of the death of a comfort woman via the internet, Jonghyeok felt a rush of pain in his heart, the same pang he felt when Grandma Chunja passed away. The image of Grandma Gwang-ok he saw a few months ago in Heilongjiang Province appeared before his eyes once more.

He couldn't tell her about Grandma Chunja's death.

They'd lived with unspeakable pain bottled up inside, yet even in their later years they were living in poverty. It was a heartrending sight. He'd promised to visit her again, but his heart was heavy as he headed home. He visited the Home Affairs Bureau and begged them again and again to look after her. Then on his way home, he looked back on Grandma Chunja's life. She wasn't his biological grandmother, but she was the only grandmother whom he loved and adored ever since he was a child.

When she'd managed to return to her hometown, rumors about how she'd become a sex toy for Japanese men or how she'd lived with a Chinese man spread throughout the town.

Chunja had been wandering the streets of Nanjing amidst the piles of corpses after the unprecedented massacre, when a Chinese man from the northeast named Wang Hai extended a hand to her. He was a fur trader who'd come to Nanjing and gotten caught up in the hellish scene of slaughter. He'd given all the money he made from the fur trade to a family to hide him for two or so months, and that was how he'd survived. He'd seen Korean slash-and-burn farmers in his hometown, and that was why he'd decided to help Chunja.

Wang Hai told her that it was fate that brought two northeasterners together in the city of that bloodbath. Like someone grasping at straws while swept up in a torrent, Chunja had followed Wang Hai home. Since he was a fur trader, she'd expected him to be somewhat rich, but his house was in a remote village in the northeast. She lived with him for eight years there, farming corn. Occasionally her husband left the village and traveled with a bundle of otter pelts as though he was going to make a fortune on them, but the few bills he came home with were never enough to lift them out of poverty.

Chunja suffered under her brutal Chinese mother-in-law with a strong northeastern accent. When her son, who was nearing forty and still wearing a cue, returned home with a woman, she seemed happy on the one hand but soon fumed tobacco smoke from a bamboo pipe as long as a walking cane and spat out, "Of all the women you could've brought home, you had to pick a Korean girl?"

Chunja's mother-in-law had a foul mouth and always stank of strong tobacco. Every sentence that came out of her mouth was followed by obscenities that insulted the listeners' ancestors to the fourth generation. And they were all directed at Chunja like a terrible rain shower. But

Chunja endured everything out of her gratitude for Wang Hai, who'd rescued her.

She did try to run away every now and then. The skin on her forehead broke once when her mother-in-law had flung her bamboo pipe at her. Wang Hai—and his mother in particular—didn't let her leave. The last time she ran away at night, Wang Hai had chased her to the train station but let her go after all. Chunja hadn't given birth for eight years, and Wang Hai and his mother had been thinking of taking a second wife. After being raped countless times in the never-ending hell of her life as a comfort woman, Chunja was unable to bear children.

And so Chunja returned home after eight years. She'd left with a heart full of dreams, but she'd returned a wreck, shedding the shattered and crushed pieces of those dreams behind her.

Her hometown was full of the joy of liberation after Japan's surrender, but people greeted her with cold gazes. When Chunja finally returned home, her mother, Kkeutsun, who was always gruff and blunt, looked at her as if she were looking at a neighbor's cow on the other side of the fence. She stared at her for a while like a weak, starved beast of the field, then, without a word, she handed Chunja a kitchen knife.

Watching Chunja's face still wet with tears turn pale with shock, Kkeutsun said, "Go on, slash your throat, or… if you don't want to do that, then go cut some wild vegetables and herbs from the mountains. Don't just stand there like you're nailed to the ground."

As Chunja headed out—or was nearly thrown out of the house by her mother, who spared her no greeting— she looked back and saw Kkeutsun wiping her tears away with a corner of her grimy skirt. But when her eyes met Chunja's, she made a fist with her hand and punched the air a few times.

Her hometown was ablaze with dazzling azaleas as usual.

Chunja noticed the mass grave at the town entrance. It was once again covered with azalea branches. The grave looked like a huge flower wreath. When she looked over at the smaller grave near the big one, Chunja froze in her steps on the hill with the dirtied kitchen knife still in her hand.

There was a new grave near Pastor Jang's grave. It lay between the azalea bushes that blossomed scarlet in regret and sorrow, and a man who had just bowed to pay his respects at the grave stood up and stopped short at the sight of Chunja.

It was Jang Mo-se. He had a pair of glasses on the bridge of his nose, but other than that he still looked neat and trim. He was wearing a black clerical suit with his shirt buttoned all the way up to the collar, and the spring sunlight reflected off the button on his collar.

Their eyes met. The spring sunlight that grew stronger by day was shining on top of their heads like acupuncture needles. As though a ray of sun had touched the right spot, they stood frozen and stared at each other.

Chunja noticed a pale-faced six- or seven-year-old girl standing next to Mo-se, holding the hem of his clothes, watching Chunja with her big eyes.

When Chunja had managed to return to her hometown after eight years, Jang Mo-se was already married with a daughter. But his wife, who had also been a member of a church choir, passed away soon after giving birth from a postpartum stroke. Having buried her on the hill of his own hometown, Mo-se had been leading a solitary life, raising his daughter all by himself.

Mo-se was shocked to see Chunja, who had appeared after years of absence, harboring terrible pain and secrets. He was able to assume a lot from her sorry and despondent appearance. Mo-se decided to take care of Chunja, who had lost her faith. And he wanted his daughter to receive motherly love once more.

Yet unable to let go of her grief and pain, Chunja downright rejected Mo-se's request, despite having adored him in the past. Several years passed before she finally accepted Mo-se's generous hand.

For the first ten years of their marriage, the two of them suffered the public humiliation of being labeled a "toy for Japanese troops" and a "Jesus lover" and dragged through the streets with conical hats on their heads and worn-out shoes around their necks. But the two of them lived together until the 1980s, when Grandpa Mo-se passed away after suffering a stroke. For the first time, Jonghyeok learned the truth about his family's history— that his mother was Chunja's stepdaughter.

Alone, Jonghyeok walked through the streets lined with jade-colored rooftops that emanated imposing auras.

"They say that when a white heron put its injured leg into the hot water gushing from a crevice, it was completely healed. That's how these hot springs came to be famous."

In his head, Jonghyeok could hear the voice tender like a breeze brushing against grass. It was Haruko's voice that he missed so much.

First day of spring—
I keep thinking about
the end of autumn.

Enveloped in longing for Haruko, he quietly mumbled Basho's haiku to himself.

"Natsume Soseki's city – Matsuyama."
"Japan's Shakespeare: Natsume Soseki."
There were placards hanging from buildings and trees lining the streets in celebration of the hundredth anniversary of the writer's death.

Jonghyeok noticed that the events planned for the centennial anniversary had brought foreign visitors to town. He watched with pleasant surprise at the waves of crowds gathering to celebrate Soseki in this small town with hot springs.

Continuously questioning one's true identity while expressing universal human emotions, Soseki's works transcended time to become classics and were growing ever brighter over time. They not only captured readers of his own time but also modern-day bibliophiles. Moreover, as an exemplary enlightened intellectual and a modern man, who sharply criticized the limits of Meiji Japan as it pursued modernization and Westernization, Soseki had become the future of Japan.

Jonghyeok idly walked through the streets packed with regional specialty goods shops, food stalls, seafood restaurants, udon noodle shops, and handicrafts stores. Rickshaw drivers in uniforms with the hot springs logo were running through the streets carrying guests on their rickshaws and shouting, "*Sumimasen, doshite kudasai* (Excuse me, please clear the way)!" while people standing at food stalls eating Botchan *dan-go* made his mouth water.

He remembered getting a taste of the sweet Botchan *dan-go*, which the protagonist in Soseki's novel enjoyed. He recalled the image of Haruko laughing with her dimpled face. That day when the sweet taste had spread pleasantly through his body…

Jonghyeok's footsteps eventually stopped by the Botchan Karakuri Clock. The clock tower that appeared in Natsume Soseki's novel *Botchan*. There were hordes of people in front of the clock tower, where the characters from Soseki's novel appeared one by one at the top of the hour. The elaborate clocktower that cost one billion yen to build was now a landmark in Matsuyama along with the hot springs, and it was becoming even more famous with the hundredth anniversary of the writer's death.

 Around the clocktower were models dressed in *yukata* like the characters in the novel, walking around with beautiful Japanese parasols covered in floral designs. Tourists from all around the world were busy taking pictures with those models with the clocktower in the background. Chinese tourists made up the largest share of foreigners. Jonghyeok heard people speaking familiar Chinese here and there. Everyone was nervously checking their cell phone clocks and watches. They were waiting for the characters of *Botchan* to appear from the clock at the top of the hour.

Jonghyeok also kept on checking his cell phone clock and lifting his head to look at the clocktower. In the eyes of the people who were anxiously waiting, the clock hands seemed to be moving slower than ever before.

Jonghyeok took out a selfie stick from his backpack.

Since he was alone, he had to use it to take pictures of himself and the surroundings. Even though he had a new cell phone with upgraded camera functions, Jonghyeok wasn't excited at all. The loneliness inherent in having to use a selfie stick seemed to be pushing out the pleasure of visiting a famous attraction and was making a part of his heart ache.

He decided to get a photograph with a model in a *yukata* and the clocktower in the background like everyone else was doing. The models continued to move through the crowd of visitors, smiling brightly. There was no sign of annoyance on the faces of these people who were chosen to promote the landmark in their hometown. Their traditional attire and hairdo, complete with their smiling faces, resembled traditional Japanese wooden dolls.

Eventually, Jonghyeok's turn came, and he walked up to one of the models. He was drawn to her by the parasol she was holding above her head—it was printed with the woodblock print artist Katsushika Hokusai's *The Great Wave off Kanagawa*.

"Could I get a picture with you?" he asked the model.

"*Hai, yorokonde* (yes, I'd be delighted)!"

The model lowered her parasol, revealing her face. At that moment, the selfie stick fell from Jonghyeok's hand. A wave of surprise bigger than *The Great Wave off Kanagawa* rose in his heart. The beautiful woman in a *yukata* with a cherry blossom print and a parasol with *The Great Wave off Kanagawa* was none other than Haruko.

Haruko had come home in time for the celebration of the anniversary of Natsume Soseki's death and volunteered to be a model during the celebration.

"Haruko?"

"Jonghyeok?"

It felt as though time had stopped. Everything seemed to have stopped, including the Botchan Ressha that was running across the street, the busy footsteps of the rickshaw drivers carrying tourists, the wind chimes that were tinkling on top of the sliding doors to the shops, the flapping placards printed with the face of Soseki, the swaying front paw of the *maneki-neko* on top of the counter at the *udon* noodle shop, the flowery parasols twirling above the models' shoulders, and even the trickle of water from the hose that fell into the footbath.

Tears welled up in Haruko's eyes. Jonghyeok could

see the reflection of the Botchan Karakuri Clock in her watery eyes. Jonghyeok stepped up close to her and wiped the tears from her cheeks, and Haruko threw aside her parasol and melted into his embrace. Jonghyeok pulled his arms around her shoulders and hugged her closely.

They heard applause all around them. Some people whistled. As if they were blessing Jonghyeok and Haruko's reunion, people clapped and cheered.

Ding! The clock tolled above their heads. The sound of the clock bell shook the plaza, and people exclaimed as they grew closer to the tower. Finally, the hands on the Botchan Karakuri Clock were heading toward the top of the hour.

Excited, the tourists began to count down in unison.

"Nine! Eight! Seven! Six!"

Jonghyeok and Haruko joined in, "Four! Three! Two! One!"

A new era was beginning.

Endnotes

1 Natsume, Soseki. *Botchan (Master Darling)*. Translated by Yasotaro Morri. Project Gutenberg, 2012, 193.

2 Natsume, Soseki. *Botchan (Master Darling)*. Translated by Yasotaro Morri. Project Gutenberg, 2012, 49.

3 Natsume, Soseki. Botchan (Master Darling). Translated by Yasotaro Morri. Project Gutenberg, 2012, 123.

4 Translated by Steven D. Carter. In *Traditional Japanese Poetry: An Anthology* by Steven D. Carter. Stanford University Press, 1991, 338.

5 Translated by Robert Hass at https://allpoetry.com/How-admirable.

6 Translated by Harold Gould Henderson. In *The Classic Tradition of Haiku: An Anthology*, edited by Faubion Bowers. Dover Publications,1996, 5.

7 Translated by Robert Hass. In *The Essential Haiku: Versions of Basho, Buson, & Issa*, edited by Robert Hass. Ecco, 1994, 81.

8 Translated by David G. Lanoue. In *Issa and Being Human,* by David G. Lanoue. HaikuGuy.com, 2017, 228.

9 Translated by Lucien Stryk. In *On Love and Barley: Haiku of Basho,* by Matsuo Basho. Translated by Lucien Stryk. Penguin Classics, 1986, 46.

10 Translated by Soiku Shigematsu. In *Zen Haiku: Poems and Letters of Natsume Soseki,* by Soseki Natsume, Soiku Shigematsu, et al. Weatherhill, 1994, 92.

11 Translated by Robert Hass at https://allpoetry.com/First-day-of-spring.

12 Natsume, Soseki. *Botchan (Master Darling).* Translated by Yasotaro Morri. Project Gutenberg, 2012, 49.